My Life in Rugby

Contents

Acknowledgements

Only when you look back over your career do you begin to realise just how many people helped it all to happen and how much you owe individuals. I know I was very lucky to have met so many people whose encouragement and assistance guided my life in rugby, and helped give me a purpose and direction I might not have had without them.

I certainly owe a big thank-you to Roger Goode, the PE master at Bishop Hannon School in Cardiff. Roger loved his rugby, and possessed that rare gift of being able to impart knowledge and encouragement with no apparent effort. He spent a lot of his spare time with me, and his enthusiasm and faith in my ability put me on the road. All players need motivation and I certainly got that, too, from Alun Ford, who coached me when I played for Cardiff Schools.

I also owe a great debt to my mother's brother, Vincent. From the age of eight, I had Vincent's support and help. He was a constant presence, come rain or shine, hardly missing a match in which I played. Uncle Vincent was always the one who took me to matches, providing pocket money, kit and encouragement with paternal benevolence. He said he enjoyed doing it, and I hope he did, because without him I don't think I'd have played as many matches as a youngster, or learned so much.

I found many valuable and lasting friendships, too, within the Cardiff club, and none more so than Albert Francis and Bill Hardiman, who were not only groundsmen but genuine and undemanding supporters whom I came to rely upon for friendship and advice. I owe Albert especially – he taught me to play golf.

I was fortunate, too, in my employers; first, Tommy Foley,

not only for letting me have so much time off to play, and later my present 'boss' Neil O'Halloran, chairman of Erection & Welding Group of Cardiff, who guided my career in more senses than one.

I also owe much, in so many ways, to my parents and to Bert and Eileen, my wife's parents, with whom I identify in a real family sense. The biggest sacrifices made on my behalf, though, were those of my wife. Susan, like many a rugby wife, put up with much and rarely grumbled at the many months of absence that my rugby career demanded. Whenever things went wrong, I relied heavily on Susan's cheerfulness and support, and I know that I wouldn't be where I am today without her.

I am indebted to rugby historian John Jenkins, of Bow Street, Dyfed, for his painstaking research in both Rugby Union and Rugby League, and to Paul Rees, of the *Western Mail*, who because of his interest in all affairs concerning Cardiff RFC, was able to provide many valuable statistics. In rugby, unlike cricket, statistics are not a necessary by-product of the sport, but Paul was successful in convincing me that facts have become increasingly important in the modern game and for the modern player.

I am also grateful to my fellow-countryman Trevor Foster, of Bradford Northern, for providing much background material about that great Rugby League club and the history of Odsal Stadium, my new stamping ground. At Bradford I had to learn not only a new game, but a new language, and Trevor proved to be a fine coach in both respects.

1

New Start

After a week in which lashing rain, flooded rivers and gale-force winds made us all believe winter had arrived early, the Big Day, thankfully, was perfect. Sunday, 31 August 1986, the day of my first home championship match for Bradford Northern, was one of those balmy, sunny, lazy summer days that your parents tell you they always used to enjoy.

A few fluffy white clouds drifted across a blue Bradford sky, and the Odsal Stadium pitch, lush emerald green and manicured to perfection for the visit of Widnes, was an example of the groundsman's art.

'Lovely, it is,' appraised Albert Francis, Cardiff's groundsman, who had come up for the match and who is always ready to pay tribute to his fellow tradesmen.

The tail-end of Hurricane Charlie, which had created widespread havoc with an unfriendly and unseasonal visit earlier in the week, teasingly gusted down-pitch, helping the side attacking with it but posing no serious problem to the defenders. Widnes – a shade provocatively, I thought – wore red, darker than Llanelli scarlet but hinting at the menace of latter-day Rugby Union rivalry. Good, though; it promised to give the contest that little extra edge.

Odsal's impressively handsome new stand and the steep, high-tiered terracing, with the compulsory safety-conscious crash barriers and clearly defined spectator walkways, soon began to fill up; beneath them, in spanking new changing-rooms, twenty-six players and reserves donned boots, jocks and jerseys and went through their pre-match preparations, each following his own private mental ritual. Outside in the sunshine, knots of jovial old-timers, long-standing supporters with flasks of tea and

1

sandwiches, made their leisurely way to the best viewpoints, mingling with family groups – Dad and Mum with kids in newly knitted scarves and hats of white, black, amber and red. The police, some of them women constables, strolled unconcernedly in the background in short-sleeve order, doubtless relieved that duty hadn't posted them to less convivial crowd entrances and terraces. The club, with typical over-confidence, expected a large audience. Certainly the crowd seemed to be in excess of 6,000 when the referee John Holdsworth, from Leeds, blew the first whistle of Bradford's new season. Officially, 4,700 came and paid. Some of Northern's directors expressed disappointment at the comparatively small attendance; others were philosophical. 'Early days yet,' said one. A rugbyman's optimism is the same, whether it's League or Union.

Not many would have got in free, in any event. Gate security was markedly tight and efficient. If you didn't have a ticket, you had to pay. 'I'm John Basnett, of Widnes,' said the Great Britain right wing to one gateman. 'Got yer ticket?' 'No, 'fraid not,' replied John, trying to explain that he had travelled independently of the rest of the Widnes team. 'Sorry, lad, you can't come in without a ticket.' The gateman stood his ground. The likelihood of John failing to get in and Widnes having to take the field without him was averted when he spotted a Widnes official and called him over for the identity parade. Status was confirmed with understanding nods and smiles all round; Widnes, old rivals of Northern, wouldn't have *that* as an excuse if they lost.

The family was there, too, with visitors from Cardiff, and a crowd of friends from other parts of Wales. Their cheerful bonhomie, nasal Kar-diff and softer, lyrical western Welsh, mingled easily and naturally with broad Bradford.

'Up t'watch some real rugby, then?' a Northern supporter teased as the Welsh contingent took their seats in the stand. 'Dead right, boy. Up to watch Holmesy, we are!' Everybody laughed. It was that kind of day, quippy and good-natured, a genuine rugby ambience; the welcome's no different whether it's the Arms Park or Odsal.

Eileen and Bert, my parents-in-law, sat side by side while the rest of the family distributed themselves willy-nilly in the stand's comfortable, well-spaced-out red seats. Susan's brother Paul, his voice hoarse from the previous evening's singsong, relied for close vocal support on brother-in-law Tommy, his mate Mickey, and Cy, who's a Pontypridd fan through and through. Ursula, Susan's sister, patiently explained the finer points of the League game to her children, Tommy Junior and Rachel, who frowned deeply, not quite understanding why Uncle Terry was wearing a No. 7 shirt and not a No. 9.

'Which ones are the Baddies, Mam?' enquired Rachel. 'Widnes, the ones in red,' whispered Ursula, wondering whether there were any Widnes supporters close by. 'Come on the Goodies!' yelled Northern's newest and youngest fan.

Helen Davies and Carole Donovan sat with my wife Susan, who was nervous as a sparrow, a seating arrangement which diplomatically enabled their husbands, Gareth and Alun, to rub shoulders, swap opinions and compare the way Cardiff played when all three of us played together at the Arms Park. Albert Francis, as is his way, felt obliged to pass on long-standing knowledge of local rules to his pal Greg Thomas, who was taking a few days off from his bowling duties for Glamorgan. Greg, anxiously awaiting the announcement of England's tour party to Australia (alas, he failed to make the team), was watching his first live Rugby League match, as were John Jenkins, a rugby researcher from Dyfed, and his sister Ann. Both were impressed by the sustained speed and skills that are somehow more obvious than in Union. Ann reserved judgement: 'I enjoyed it,' she said later. 'It was very good. And exciting, my word. But I'm not sure I'd prefer it to Union.' Loyal to the national game, those Welsh girls.

The point was that they were all there, lending moral as well as vocal support. They all understood, of course, how important the day was for me, tangibly more important than my appearances at the back-end of the previous season. I'd prefer to think that those first matches didn't count, that in a way they didn't really take place – a sort of recurring dream, or perhaps a nightmare – for I dislocated my left shoulder twice, against Swinton and Batley, ending up both times in the Yorkshire

3

Clinic in Bingley. These misadventures gave the cynics a field day, and caused many others to suspect I had made the wrong move in switching codes. It was one of the most depressing times of my life, not so much because of the injuries – an ever-present possibility for any participant in a physical-contact sport – but because my new life, my new career, had got off to the worst kind of start. Although both injuries were entirely accidental, I still felt I'd let so many people down.

During the nine months I was sidelined, I had plenty of chance to come to terms with misfortune. Fortunately the operation to strengthen the shoulder and the subsequent rehabilitation had gone very well; my confidence was back, and after a lot of hard training and a couple of pre-season warm-up matches, I felt I was ready to start again. The match with Widnes, therefore, took on added significance; not only was it to be a proving ground for so many people, including myself, but, above all, it was an early opportunity to repay the faith and confidence of the Bradford directors and staff. Northern's spectators, too, without whom we wouldn't have a club, were entitled to some evidence that the previous season's highly publicised signing had not been all ballyhoo, and that there was something I could contribute.

Fortunately, it was no soft pipe-opener. Widnes were good opposition, and a club with whom Northern had a score or two to settle. In recent years, they had enjoyed the whiphand over us, and although such memories probably irk supporters far more than players, it was added incentive. As the new boy at Northern, I obviously wanted to do well personally, but I was also keen to be part of a quality team performance. In the circumstances, it could hardly be just another match.

Although other people's expectations of you are important, what matters even more is what you expect of yourself, what you are prepared to give. That effort is relative and individual; no two people think or behave alike. My contribution on the field, by good fortune, is entirely instinctive, and I've never been over-concerned with pre-match psychology or rituals. I couldn't play any game unless I gave everything to it. I simply do it without analysing it – like switching on to automatic pilot.

Even so, given my experiences, I can't pretend that I didn't

4

feel a little nervous. It was not the butterflies-in-the-belly or the tension you feel before going out to play, say, an international at the Arms Park, where the passion and anticipation outside in the stadium naturally permeate through to the changing-rooms. You're on a high from the moment you wake up on an international morning, and by the time you have gone through all the preparation and have actually taken the field, you are really flying. The apprehension I now felt was not at all the same.

Understandably, the adrenalin took a little longer to course through the veins for this match against Widnes. My preparation was calculatedly different. Possibly because I realised how important the new start was, I made a conscious effort to play everything down. I felt good mentally and physically. I knew I was fit, and that all the work I'd done with weights and regular cross-country running, which topped up my normal twice-a-week club training, would stand me in good stead. The pre-season warm-up matches had been valuable, too, both for testing out the shoulder in match conditions and for improving my still scanty tactical knowledge of Rugby League.

I only began to 'switch on' and think seriously about the match late in the morning, four hours or so before kick-off, when I took my golden Labrador, Shar, for her usual romp around the fields of the village of Clifton where I now live. I was pleased that it was going to be fine and dry for the match, conditions which suited the expressive fluid game Northern preferred to play. Shar was well behaved that morning too. For a change, she didn't chase the cows.

Back home, meanwhile, those of the 'gang' from Wales who were not hung-over tried hard to act unconcerned. 'Just another match, isn't it?' . . . '*Of course* he'll be all right.' . . . 'DON'T mention injuries.' . . . It was flawless Basil Fawlty. I pretended not to notice.

Although Susan and I had managed to put up some of the family in our house, most of my visitors had stayed the night just across the road, at my 'local', the Black Horse Inn, a small hotel which has been converted from a bevy of attractive old Yorkshire stone cottages, and which is run with homely efficiency by Pat and Brian Hubbard. Brian proudly dispenses a splendid pint

of Castle Ale ('It's Cassle, not Carsle,' he corrected me almost
the first time I called there). He is also well versed in both rugby
codes, for although once a captain of nearby Cleckheaton Rugby
Union club (first club, incidentally, of another local lad, England
centre Jeff Butterfield), he also appreciates the appeal of Rugby
League, is very knowledgeable about the game and the players,
and is often a spectator at Odsal. Brian and Pat were among the
first Yorkshire people to make Susan and me feel at home. Ta,
both.

I told everyone I had to get to the ground early, but that they
had plenty of time for a smashing, leisurely Sunday lunch at the
Black Horse. Pat's Yorkshire puddings are the size of Bob
Norster's fist, and, I hinted, the tastiest in the West Riding. I also
mentioned as an alternative that the Commercial Inn – The
Woolpack, of 'Emmerdale Farm' fame – was just up the road, at
Esholt. Soap outpointed Yorkshire puddings. The Woolpack
got the vote. By the time I was pulling into the Odsal car park,
they were probably on their second pints of Whitbread's and
wondering when Seth Armstrong was going to appear.

A Rugby League player (unlike most in Rugby Union) only
has to take himself to the ground for a home match. All his kit,
boots, crisply laundered jersey and stockings, are there in the
changing-rooms waiting for him, tied up in a neat, compact
bundle like a Christmas present. Very little else differs from a
Union dressing-room. As players arrive they chat and joke, talk
about the weather or suggest a new watering-hole after the
match. At Cardiff, often enough, there'd be a big pre-match
team talk and a brisk foot-stamping warm-up. This doesn't
happen at Northern or, come to that, any League club.
Everyone has been primed for the job at hand at the previous
training session. Consequently the coach, Barry Seabourne,
says very little in the minutes before kick-off; no passionate
exhortations, just a few reassuring words here and there. Much
is left to self-motivation. The players know what they have to do;
neither the coach nor the club captain needs to emphasise it. I
think the players prefer it that way.

The most active people in the changing-room, oddly enough,
are the nominated match reserves, who help with the massage

and rub-downs. Every player, whether he is a so-called star or not, has this job whenever he is a reserve, and I believe these little things do much to build a good team spirit. As match time approaches, a relatively quiet, reflective period takes over; each player is left to his own devices, his own mental preparation.

The obvious difference between Union and League changing-rooms is the availability of protective padding. Some players don their shoulder pads like medieval knights putting on their armour before battle, refusing to take the field without them. Others regard them as at best a nuisance and at worst a hindrance. So far I haven't padded up, not because of make-do or bravado, but simply because it takes getting used to and is part of the learning process. One day perhaps I'll take it for granted.

Barry Seabourne came up to me just before we left the dressing-room. 'Good luck,' he said reassuringly. 'Go out there and enjoy yourself. Remember, you've got nothing to prove.'

I nodded my appreciation and understanding, and trotted out into the sunshine with the rest of the team. The season was about to kick-off, and I felt, with luck, we would do well. Everybody had worked very hard in the pre-season preparation, and confidence was high: we could and would beat Widnes. We did.

My contribution was not exactly spectacular, but probably I tried that extra bit harder. Gaps very rarely appear in Rugby League, and when they do, instinct takes over. A couple of runs into space, and with support on either side it was comparatively easy. Two passes brought two early tries. Even a couple of subsequent 'welcome to Rugby League' clouts from Widnes failed to dampen my enthusiasm, and although I began to puff a bit towards the end, I thoroughly enjoyed myself. It was a great feeling, made better, of course, because we won and won well.

Afterwards, the Press probed me for my reactions. I greeted them with 'I'm sorry you didn't have an injury to report about this time'. Most of them appreciated the intended humour and laughed but, sadly, one reporter interpreted my remark in a rather different way. Ray French, writing in *Today*, reckoned my 'ill-conceived greeting' had 'soured' my come-back and accused me of having a chip on my shoulder. Later, Ray – a much-respected figure in Rugby League – rang me to apologise for the article. I was not bothered by it and I accepted his apology without reservations, although I was slightly baffled by his explanation that someone in the *Today* office had inserted the offending words and that he in fact had not written them. Perhaps we both need new script-writers.

One thing was certain: all my visitors up from Wales seemed happy enough. Once Bradford had discovered that there were a few 'special' guests among them – Gareth Davies and Alun Donovan, both Welsh internationals, and Greg Thomas, an England Test cricketer – they went out of their way to make them officially welcome. All three were invited to the private after-match reception for the players, directors and match sponsors. The irony of the situation was not lost on Gareth, for after all it must have been unique for such an invitation to be extended to – and accepted by – a future Barbarians committee-man. Knowing his impish humour, I wouldn't be surprised if Gareth was wondering if it was all a fiendish Northern plot and that he and Alun might be compromised in some way. He might even get an offer! He'd have been disappointed, though. Northern's directors were no more than politely interested in their two Rugby Union visitors, for the centre of attraction undoubtedly was Greg, and most of the chat centred on cricket.

Meantime the rest of the clan were enjoying the conviviality of the adjacent Northern players' bar – none more so than Cy, who felt he couldn't let the opportunity pass without getting as many autographs as possible. He was absolutely delighted that Jim Mills breezed in, not only prepared to write a good-luck message on Cy's programme but more than happy to discuss Northern's newest Welsh signing. 'We're all delighted Terry's come through today,' said Jim, 'but he's not a Rugby League scrum-half. I'm sure Northern'll turn him into a loose forward – he's a natural for the position.'

Cy was a bit nonplussed by Jim's views. Obviously he respected the opinions of this revered Rugby League player; but at the same time – incredibly as far as Cy was concerned – Jim had touched on heresy by casting doubt on my scrum-half ability. 'I can't believe Jim meant it,' Cy told me. 'It's only an opinion,' I replied. 'Just because Jim says something will happen it doesn't necessarily mean it will.'

Obviously I was intrigued, and flattered, to learn how Jim Mills saw my Rugby League career panning out. Jim, now a director of Widnes, is one of the most respected figures in the game. As an ex-Cardiff player, and one of those Welshmen who went north and stayed to be assimilated into the life and culture of Rugby League country, his observations counted for a lot. It will be interesting to see if his prediction comes true.

To say that Jim – still a trim 6 foot 4 inches and not far off his playing weight of 17 stone – had a chequered Rugby League career is an understatement. Fine forward though he was, he was not the most disciplined of fellows; he was sent off fifteen times and, during three years' playing in Australia, he was dismissed another five times. He is the only player to have been twice sent off when playing for Wales. He was big, tough and rough, but he was also a player of tremendous ability, a thundering great tackler and an excellent passer. Had he stayed in Rugby Union there is no doubt he would have been capped by Wales.

Aberdare-born, Jim came to prominence when, after joining my old club, Cardiff, he captained Wales Youth against France and England in 1962–3. He played only sixteen matches for Cardiff, signing for Halifax in 1964, when he was twenty. His early League career, like mine, was marred by injury and it was over a year before he was able to make the first of thirty-eight first-team appearances for Halifax. By 1968 he had moved on to Salford, but he played only five times for them before he signed for Bradford Northern, and in his two seasons at Odsal he played fifty-two matches as an open-side prop. He played alongside another of Northern's Welsh captures, Terry Price, for Wales against England in 1969, and then turned down the chance to tour Australia with Great Britain in 1970 because he had signed for North Sydney on a three-year contract. He was not to play for Great Britain until 1974, when he made three appearances; and he played in three further Tests in 1978 and 1979.

By 1972 Jim had joined another Welshman, John Warlow, at Widnes, where his outstanding play helped that club to fourteen finals, including the famous victory in the Challenge Cup over

Warrington at Wembley in 1975. The try Jim scored in that match is still spoken of admiringly in League clubs. He appeared in two other Wembley finals, the defeat by Leeds in 1977 and victory again in 1979 against Wakefield Trinity. His League career came to an end after he injured a knee against Bradford Northern in 1980.

The little party we planned that evening to celebrate a memorable day for everyone was marred only by the fact that thieves had broken into Greg Thomas's Volvo in the club car park and had made off with a number of items, including a set of golf clubs. Albert Francis, Greg's travelling companion from Wales, suffered more: his travelling case and all his clothes, including a lot of his golf gear, were missing, which mortified him because a day on the golf course was scheduled for the next day. I called the police, who held out little hope of catching the villains and retrieving the stolen goods. Funny thing, Greg didn't seem to mind too much. He seemed much more interested in one of the constables, a very attractive young lady who, coincidentally, had been on duty at the match earlier in the day. Greg pressed her for her telephone number. 'Try 999,' she suggested, dismissing him with a smile.

Next day, we still played golf, Albert quite happy to strut around the Bingley St Ives course like Charlie Chaplin in an odd assortment of borrowed gear. He paired up with my brother-in-law Tommy against Greg and myself. Modesty forbids my revealing the outcome, except to say that Greg played tremendously. 'He's an animal,' Albert ruefully remarked of his driving. As we approached the eighteenth hole, Cy came running up from the car park. 'Just heard on the car radio – David Bishop's been sent to prison for a month,' he blurted out. We all knew 'Bish', who had appeared in court charged with assaulting a Newbridge player during a match. Although we feared the worst, the news was shattering.

'Never,' said Tommy incredulously.

'A bloody shame,' declared Albert.

'He doesn't deserve that,' was my first reaction, although I had mixed feelings about the whole affair.

At the time it seemed a tragedy that Bishop was in court at all.

He was a naughty boy, no doubt. But it seemed to me that his offence should have been dealt with not by the police, or a criminal court, but by the sporting body involved, the Welsh Rugby Union. Not that I condone violence in any way; it has to be stamped out, no mistake. However, it really is up to the clubs to sort out excessively violent players. If they have any, they shouldn't play them.

When his sentence was suspended on appeal and the WRU then slapped a year's ban on him, we all guessed that he'd automatically try fresh pastures in Rugby League. None of us was surprised, though, that the League scotched that possibility by announcing that none of their clubs could negotiate with him until the WRU suspension was completed. All in all, it was a very sad story for both Rugby Union and Rugby League. In cases like this, there are no winners.

2
Signing

Although I didn't fully appreciate it at the time, my life was changed forever in the week before Wales played Fiji at Cardiff on 9 November 1985. I was to captain Wales that day, and naturally I was engrossed with the match and the accompanying responsibilities, when the telephone rang at the office. It was Tuesday, 5 November.

'Hello, Terry. This is Barry Stamper of Bradford Northern. We're interested in signing you.'

I had met Barry, but with my mind on other matters, the call was a bombshell. At first I couldn't take it all in. I could only mutter an odd word or two as Barry outlined the offer. It was a few minutes before I fully registered the importance of what he was saying. Eventually I told him I *was* interested but pointed out that I couldn't think about anything at that moment, except captaining Wales. Politely, I asked Barry if we could talk at some future date. He said he understood, and that he'd ring back next week, after the match, if that was suitable. I agreed and replaced the receiver, still in a daze. The die was cast.

There was nothing new for me in being offered terms to turn Rugby League; this was in fact the fourth time during my career that I had been approached. One enquiry had been from Bradford two years earlier. But this latest offer had come at the precise moment in my life when I was considering retirement from international rugby. Indeed, I was preparing to play against Fiji tinkering with the notion that it might be my last appearance for Wales. I had already decided privately that I would not be available for the World Cup in the summer of 1987, and, that being so, it would have been unrealistic and possibly unfair to Wales to have made myself eligible for the earlier

Championship matches. I suppose Barry's call removed any lingering doubts about retiring from international rugby, although at the time I was much further from seriously considering his offer than he might have appreciated. There were many things to weigh up, and I was not going to rush into anything. Circumspection had always been the Holmes watchword, and I was not about to change the habit of a lifetime. The Fiji match had top priority . . . for the moment.

According to a strict interpretation of the Rugby Union laws, I suppose I was risking being branded a professional because I should not even have been talking to Bradford Northern, although the approach came from them. Nor was it the first time that I had risked the full wrath of the WRU descending on my head. I had previously discussed possibilities with Salford and Cardiff Blue Dragons as well as Bradford. All those discussions, for obvious reasons, were conducted in great secrecy, although on none of those occasions did I feel guilty, or underhand, or that I was breaking the law. I never believed for a moment that one could be professionalised merely by talking. The Rugby Union authorities must surely realise that they could never make such a charge stick, so why they have included this specific warning in their rules I do not understand. It makes little sense. In my view, players who might hesitate, for instance, about playing in a Rugby League trial are never going to be frightened of talking to Rugby League clubs because of a few words in the handbook. No court in the land would uphold such a ban on players.

From time to time rumours are spread of 'famous' Rugby Union players appearing in Rugby League trials under aliases. They may be true, I don't know. What I do know is that, contrary to speculation, I had never played any form of Rugby League until I joined Bradford. Yet for some reason, which has always mystified me, I have been associated with Rugby League in one form or another for most of my career. What I do admit to, of course, is *talking* to Rugby League clubs. Approaches have been made, and I have listened.

Salford, that great Lancashire club where David Watkins

prospered, were the first to test the waters, in 1979. The businesslike approach was made on the telephone. But even if Salford had placed 100,000 crisp new fivers on my kitchen table (which they certainly didn't) I wouldn't have gone. My international career had only just begun, and to be honest I was so intent on furthering my career with Cardiff and Wales that even if they'd thrown in the Taj Mahal with the offer I wouldn't have been interested. I gave them a polite refusal, not even leaving the door ajar. They did not come back.

Bradford Northern first showed interest in me in 1984. It was untimely in the sense that the approach came shortly before I was off on tour to the Far East with Cardiff. At that precise moment I was far more interested in the tour than in a deal which ostensibly would secure my future. There was another factor. I had just been appointed captain of the club for the 1984–5 season, and that honour outweighed any financial considerations. Nonetheless, I agreed to meet Bradford's representatives. Once again, I saw no harm in discussing my future in this way.

We met at the Ladbroke Mercury Hotel just off the M4 outside Newport. It was obvious they were very serious, for they arrived rather mob-handed. I shook hands with Barry Stamper, the financial advisor to the club, Ronny Firth, the vice-chairman, and Peter Fox, who was then coach but has since moved on to Leeds. There was no 'hard sell' element in that meeting at Newport. They had come down, as was promised in the initial telephone call, to explain how Northern operated, what their plans were, and how they visualised I would fit into them. It was a very interesting and prolonged meeting, entirely business-like. We did not get as far as discussing financial terms. The stumbling-blocks were Cardiff's tour and the captaincy; but also in the back of my mind was the secret hope that I would be made captain of Wales. There was also another critical factor. Northern wanted me to sign a five-year contract. At the time that seemed a commitment for life, which, even without the other imponderables, really sabotaged the negotiations. Five years seemed to me a desperately long time. Still, I appreciated the trouble Bradford had gone to, and was flattered that they thought me worth signing. I promised I would fully consider the offer whilst on tour and that I would give them an answer on my return. This I did. The gist of that written reply was that I felt the timing was not quite right. It didn't occur to me then that I might be slamming the door on their fingers and I suppose my letter indicated that perhaps we could talk on another occasion if they were still interested.

I hope all this doesn't suggest I was playing hard to get. Although I realised that in saying 'no' there was a possibility that one day all the offers would dry up, I was simply balancing my enjoyment and love of Rugby Union against the attraction and challenge of a new game and the financial security it would give. Rugby Union won. I captained Cardiff and we had a very good season. Only one honour remained. Everyone seemed to think I was the automatic choice; everyone, that is, except me. I tingled with nervous anticipation and then, at last, it happened. I *was* made captain of Wales. So the prospect of playing Rugby League seemed very remote on 2 March 1985 when for the first time I led the Welsh team out against Scotland at Murrayfield. We won, and life at that moment seemed very good indeed. It was a moment which in a sense was my life's total fulfilment, the justification for all the effort, training and hard work, the planning, the hopes, the realisation of a cherished dream. Money and security simply didn't enter the equation.

I was, of course, very fortunate that Bradford Northern had not forgotten me. They, more than anyone, appreciated my priorities, and my sense of loyalty to a game that had been my life. Sentiment is one thing, business is another. They realised that once the glow of self-indulgence had receded I might still be interested in their offer. I admired their persistence and was very happy that they came back to the bartering table.

Many people in Rugby Union are convinced that there are a good number of so-called scouts operating in Wales on behalf of League clubs. These scouts, it is believed, work in an insidious and furtive way, cornering 'vulnerable' Rugby Union players and persuading them to change codes. Well, if so, none of them has approached me. I've not seen shadowy figures lurking outside rugby clubs with coat collars turned up, hat brims turned down and one hand on a fat wallet inside the jacket. In my experience, such people are figments of the imagination, although I concede that in the past the Rugby League scout probably operated in something of a clandestine manner out of necessity – and, if you can believe the stories told about them, in the interests of very survival.

The popular tales of these gentlemen, once unmasked, tell of their being summarily dealt with by the locals or members of the Rugby Union club. If they weren't flitting the valleys in fear of their lives or being tarred and feathered, at the very least they were roughed up a little or thrown in the river and then sent on their way. I tend to think such happenings were mildly exaggerated, helping to propagate the myth about the temptations put to players over the years. Far more likely, in my view, that the business was conducted much in the fashion as occurred when Trevor Foster became a Bradford player in 1938. Trevor tells me that representatives of various clubs approached him quite properly by letter or by calling at his home. As it happened, Trevor's particular deal was finally struck out in the open, on Newport bridge – the only touch of John Le Carré about the whole affair.

It is important to stress that no matter how badly a Rugby League club wants a Rugby Union player, it would never operate outside a well-defined code of behaviour. A League club recognises that it must at all times protect and acknowledge the player's situation in respect of Rugby Union's amateur regulations. From initial approach to discussion and final offer, if the individual does not want to play Rugby League, the club will diplomatically and quietly withdraw, and nothing more will be said. The player's career is never placed in jeopardy. No Rugby League club would have it otherwise. It should also be appreciated that these negotiations are conducted in an honest, frank and businesslike way. It is just like applying for or being interviewed for a job. There is nothing sinister about the transactions, although everyone recognises that, in order to protect the individual, negotiations have to be kept secret.

Take, for instance, the second approach made to me, on behalf of Cardiff Blue Dragons in 1982. By coincidence, I knew the go-between, Derek Ferns. Derek was no scout. I'd met him through the scrap business – he was based in Cwmbran – and we had done quite a bit of business together. Obviously he had a link with the Blue Dragons when they were formed, although I can't be sure in what capacity; he might even have been a financial backer. Either way, I suppose it was quite natural for him to talk to me about joining the Dragons. As I remember, there were few preliminaries. He said: 'David Watkins would like to talk to you about the possibility of joining the Dragons.' It was quite open, as if it were just another transaction in business. Derek was obviously not empowered to discuss details; his job was to find out if I was interested, nothing more. I agreed to meet David, then the coach of the Dragons. There was no pressure and frankly I thought that nothing would be lost by talking to him. At the least it would be fascinating to hear of his plans to bring Rugby League to Wales.

We decided to meet in Monmouth. There, in an office above a small antique shop plumb in the centre of the town, David made me a straightforward offer: £45,000. He was very keen that I sign, outlining the potential advantages that a well-known Cardiff-born player would bring to a new club based in the city. I told David that I'd like time to think about it. There were obvious attractions for me, aside from any financial considera- tion. Susan and I were shortly going away on holiday, to the Costa del Sol, and I promised David a decision when we returned.

Susan and I discussed the offer and its implications for a long time, and still I couldn't make up my mind. Eventually I took the matter to Roger Beard at Cardiff. I talked to him not as coach of Cardiff, but as a friend. I took Gareth Davies into my confidence as well. Both were considerate and helpful but neither tried to influence me one way or the other, pointing out that the decision had to be mine and mine alone. Eventually I rang David. 'I'm sorry,' I told him, 'but I don't want to join the Dragons.' The time wasn't right for me to give up Rugby Union. I wished him and the Dragons all the luck in the world. As we now know, he needed more than luck. The Dragons went to the wall. The experiment of bringing Rugby League to Wales failed.

The Dragons did very well to last as long as they did. After all, they were invading the heartland of Welsh rugby, and it was obvious they were going to have a hell of a battle to win and maintain support from a people steeped in Rugby Union. Hard as David fought to keep the Dragons going, it was always on the cards that he would fail. I don't say this with hindsight. The fear that they might collapse was high on my list of considerations when I turned down his offer.

I went to Ninian Park with my brother-in-law Tommy Foley to see the Dragons play their first match, against Salford. There were 10,000 spectators that Sunday, and the atmosphere was very good. I'm not sure what we all expected. It barely occurred to me that in different circumstances I might have been out on the pitch wearing a Dragons jersey instead of watching from the terraces. Many of the crowd, who cheered, applauded and obviously enjoyed themselves, were impressed with the high standard of play. Yet even as Tommy and I were walking away from the ground at the end, we agreed that Rugby League did not seem to possess the compelling quality to keep a Welsh crowd coming. Somehow, it didn't fit in. It didn't seem a *Cardiff* game. Sadly, we weren't the only people that day who thought in those terms. Once the novelty had worn off, the turnstiles stopped clicking. No club can survive without support, and as that dwindled, so the club lost its only means of carrying on. There were other factors, but that was the main reason for the club's demise.

As I said, I had more or less decided to end my international career after the Fiji match in 1985. There were many reasons for this, not the least that with Gareth Davies no longer on the scene, playing for Wales didn't exactly have the old appeal. In fact, few of the players left in the Welsh team were of my vintage, and although I enjoyed playing with a youngster like Jonathan Davies, I really couldn't see how I could relate to the new boys who were coming on. The truth was, my game belonged to another age, and I honestly wondered if it wasn't in Wales's best interests in building for the World Cup to forget Holmes and look immediately for someone to replace me. I think I owed Welsh rugby that, to give them a chance to find a young David Loveridge, with short, quick passes, rather than having to rely on someone like myself, whose style of play had become somewhat archaic in international terms. There was no chance that I could change that style. Long, swinging passes would be OK in Rugby League but not in the World Cup. I also remembered what had happened to J. P. R. Williams, the world's greatest full-back. He played on too long, in my view, and it was a very, very sad day for him and Welsh rugby when the selectors were forced to drop him. I didn't want that to happen to me.

The decision to end my international career therefore cleared the last reason that I might have had for resisting the challenge of Rugby League. Northern, for their part, were in a strong bargaining position for they had recently sold Ellery Hanley, the Great Britain player, to Wigan for a record £150,000. Thus both parties came together favourably disposed to a deal; the atmosphere and the timing, for a change, were right. Barry Stamper, as promised, rang me a few days after the Fiji match, and we talked for quite a long time. Finally he made me an offer that, with a few reservations, I couldn't refuse. We even discussed the possibility that I should continue to live in Cardiff and go up and down to Bradford for training and playing. Barry was aware of my close ties with Cardiff; I had already declared my reluctance to leave the city where I was born and bred. Now, after a little reflection, I decided that to stay there was neither practical nor desirable. I felt that if I was to give 100 per cent to my new club, and to earn the respect of the players, I had to move lock, stock and boots to Bradford. We agreed that the move should be high on the agenda when we met. We set the date of that meeting as 26 November, in Bradford.

By agreeing to that meeting I had partly committed myself to the most important decision of my life. Yet, curiously, I was still not absolutely certain I would sign. Although Susan and I obviously had talked over the move, and I had sought counsel from other members of my family and friends, there were certain important considerations, not the least being my job as a director of an engineering company. And I was, after all, still a Rugby Union player, with an obligation to Cardiff. So much had

19

to be discussed and done in the fortnight before I made the long trip up the motorway to Yorkshire. Once I had recovered from the bump that had put me off the field against Fiji, my first priority was to honour my playing commitments for Cardiff. I declared myself fit to play against Llanelli at Stradey Park on 23 November. Although not even I realised it at the time, it was to prove my last match as an amateur rugby player.

Stradey Park had never been a happy hunting ground for me. I played there six times but never did well there. Cardiff always found it difficult to win against Llanelli. They seemed always to be such a highly motivated side. I remember times when we were well on top but they'd find reserves from somewhere and come back to win. They are one of the great clubs in Welsh rugby, and I take my hat off to them. So Stradey was the last place I'd have chosen to play my final game of rugby. The choice, of course, wasn't mine. Circumstances dictated. As it happened, I think I played pretty well that day – at least better than on many a previous visit. Obviously, the Bradford offer was very much in mind – I had to work hard to concentrate on my game. Before and after the match reporters kept coming up and asking me about the 'rumours'. I didn't want to lie to anyone, but at the same time I couldn't admit that in three days' time I'd be negotiating to join Rugby League. The Press boys also tapped Alan Phillips, Cardiff's captain, and Roger Beard, but they didn't let on anything. It must have been a bit difficult for them and I appreciated their tact. Interestingly, I found out later that watching in the stands at Stradey that day was Terry Price, a former Scarlet and one of Bradford's major Welsh signings in the late 1960s. Terry gave sterling service to Northern but had returned to Wales to become a successful businessman.

Obviously, I would love to have played my last game for Cardiff at home, at the Arms Park. Strange, frustrating really, that I should have played my first and last match for Cardiff away from home. I remember the tremendous reception the Cardiff crowd gave Gareth Davies after he'd announced his retirement from international rugby. I'd like to have gone out the same way, saying a kind of 'thanks' to them all, but it was not to be. The next day, Monday, 25 November, I went to see Neil

O'Halloran, the chairman of my company. I asked his view about the wisdom of accepting Bradford's offer. Neil – incidentally a former Cardiff City footballer – didn't hesitate. 'You've got to do it – it's an opportunity of a lifetime.' My job, he promised, would be secure and I could take up the reins again whenever I returned to Wales. It was a marvellous gesture by Neil and, of course, another little push in the right direction.

Early on the Tuesday I set off for Bradford by car, accompanied by Tommy Foley, who is not only my brother-in-law but a good friend. It was a lovely day, warm and sunny, and with Tommy cracking jokes all the way we were there almost before I realised it. I rang Barry Seabourne, Bradford's new coach, from the Birch service station on the M62. We met at the next services stop and from there Barry took us to a pub just outside Bradford for lunch. I wasn't exactly nervous but I had no appetite. As Barry did his best to break the ice I sipped an orange juice. Tommy was loving it. For him the whole thing was a kind of conspiracy to which he was privy. He stowed away a couple of pints of Tetley's, and hardly said a word as Barry and I talked rugby – Rugby League. He told me where and how he wanted me to play (he was a former scrum-half so we had a lot in common) and by the time it came for us to leave for the formal meeting, I felt he was a friend. He was great. I liked him instantly.

It was only ten minutes from the pub to Odsal, and I just didn't know what to expect when we got there. We had a few minutes to spare and Barry took me on a short, guided tour, looking down at the stadium from the clubhouse. I was amazed. It was quite unexpected, this huge natural amphitheatre with its new stand and its cycle and speedway tracks. In my travels around the world, I'd seen many impressive stadiums, but that first view of Odsal was breathtaking, like looking down into the crater of a volcano. I realised, as soon as I had taken in that first glimpse of Rugby League's most famous ground, that I'd stepped past the point of no return. As Barry guided us into the oak-panelled Bradford committee-room, I knew that the details of the contract were going to be a formality. Even so, my excitement and apprehension had not vanished completely as Barry took me in.

Barry Stamper, Ron Firth and Paul Robinson, a club director, were waiting for us.

'Take some notes,' I whispered to Tommy. 'I might forget something. After all, it is a business meeting.' Tommy nodded and winked knowingly, convinced he was my confederate in some dark intrigue. For the next hour and a half he scribbled away furiously. Every now and then, he'd shove a scrap of paper under my nose. His writing was terrible. I couldn't understand a word.

The meeting was in fact very low-key. Everyone was relaxed and pleasant. We agreed terms, subject to a legal contract, and shook hands. Then off I went for a medical, with the club's physician, Dr Hamilton. That didn't take long, a few X-rays, etc., and it was all over. To all intents and purposes I was a Bradford Northern player. When we got outside Tommy congratulated me. 'Well done. I'm sure you've done the right thing.' The sun was still shining and I felt marvellously relaxed. Tommy was right. I had done the right thing, without a tinge of regret. As soon as I had the chance, I rang Susan. 'It's done,' I said. 'I'll be signing the formal contract next week.' She asked if there were any unexpected or unusual clauses. I said no. I told her the fee would be paid over three years and because I was relinquishing my amateur status the payments would be tax-free. With bits and pieces, the signing-on fee would amount to £80,000. I would play for Northern for three years and I'd agreed not to play 'professional rugby' for any other club after that period. Interestingly, the 'professional rugby' clause did not stipulate Rugby League or Rugby Union; Bradford were taking precautions because of mounting speculation that Rugby Union might go professional. I told them that this was extremely doubtful, but I understood their position.

Events now began to quicken. The following morning I reported to my solicitor, Martell Williams, and prepared him for the signing which was planned to take place 'live' at Yorkshire Television Studios in Leeds on Tuesday, 3 December. I also phoned Roger Beard, the Cardiff coach, and Gareth Davies. I agreed with Roger that I should announce a diplomatic injury, because he needed to explain why I was not playing that night against Maesteg and against South Wales Police on Saturday. I feigned a hamstring injury. That night BBC television, in a deft piece of anticipation, presented a profile of my career. The next day my visit to Bradford had obviously leaked; several northern papers carried the story that I had signed. It was not true, of course, and caused concern to some of the Press boys in Wales. To their queries I replied truthfully in the negative. In theory, at least, I was still a Rugby Union player. There was a big temptation to play one last match for Cardiff, but I quickly dismissed the notion. An injury could well jeopardise the signing and there was also the chance that by playing I'd professionalise everyone in the match. I was not going to take the risk either way, though I allowed myself the luxury of thinking how marvellous it would be to make a final farewell appearance at the Arms Park.

At once I assumed a low profile. There was an obvious temptation to go down to the club to watch them play South Wales Police. I put it out of my mind immediately. Instead I went training. As I was running past St David's Hospital in Canton, I spotted Tony 'Clubber' McLean, a coloured lad who'd played for Cardiff a few times. 'Hiya, Clubber,' I shouted over to him 'How did they get on?' He told me Cardiff had won – and that Bob Norster had been sent off. I was still running and it was about fifty yards before the full realisation of the Norster news struck me. I stopped. My God, poor old Bob. Being sent off meant that he'd miss the whole of the international season. The irony of the situation was like a dagger in my heart. I pondered the ups and downs of the amateur game. One moment you're flying high, the hero. The next, you can be the villain of the piece, cast aside and forgotten. It was only then, at the precise moment of comprehending the disaster which had befallen Norster, that I was absolutely convinced I was doing the right thing by signing for Bradford.

Three days later all the doubts and speculation ceased. In the full glare of a live TV show and with Martell Williams at my side and a glass of champagne in my hand, I committed myself to a new life. My Rugby Union career was officially over. My Rugby League career was about to begin.

3

Country Life

Yorkshire, after Cardiff, was a shock to the system. For someone who has lived all his life in a city, totally immersed in its urgency, its helter-skelter clamour, and loved every minute of it, I found the leisurely pace and the tranquillity of the countryside took an awful lot of getting used to. During the first few months there, it was like being stranded on an uninhabited island miles from any kind of civilisation, a mind-dulling contrast to the comparatively hectic lifestyle Susan and I had enjoyed in Cardiff. We also had to adjust to the crisp, clean air, which was as tiring and energy-sapping as if we lived 5,000 feet above sea-level. There were so many contrasts, in the beginning, that both of us had grave doubts – usually unspoken – that we'd ever adapt, physically or psychologically. I even began to wonder whether my move to play for Bradford Northern might be the biggest mistake of my life.

'You'll get used to it . . . You'll learn to love the life.' There was plenty of reassurance. People went out of their way to be helpful, friendly and welcoming, as if they realised we were having acclimatisation problems. And so it proved. Before either of us was really aware of it, we had adjusted and – more to my surprise than Sue's – I found I *liked* the country life.

When my Rugby League days are over, however, I still intend to return to Cardiff and indulge in the city life again. I'll never lose that sense of belonging there, and being a part of the place. The feeling is ingrained, and beautiful and diverse though Yorkshire is, nothing will change my deep-rooted affection for the town in which I was born.

But in the meantime, when in Rome . . . it's the rural life for me. In fact, I'm much taken with the idea of adopting the style and life of a country gent. I don't know where this yearning comes from, considering I'm a townie through and through, and that the only stretch of grass with which I have been truly familiar is the Arms Park pitch. I think I must have the temperament for the countryside. The wellies and the weather-proofed hunting jacket are compulsory, of course. All I need now, I think, is a good, stout walking-stick and some coaching in rural folk-lore (a couple of James Herriot novels should do the trick there) to complete the transformation. Might make sense, too, to order a couple of tickets for the next Game Fair. I'm even thinking of buying myself a shotgun and a rod; just the tackle for one man and his Labrador to go a-roaming through dingle and dale. Now *what's* the Welsh word for 'squire'?

We were lucky that Bradford Northern found us a home in Clifton, a little village of old, mostly stone-built cottages nestling in the foothills of the Pennines. There are obvious advantages in being close to the big cities in the area, like Bradford itself, and Leeds. Yet away from the towns, living in a village such as Clifton, which is hemmed in by meadows and pasture, you seem to be in another world, gentler and softer, just like the landscape. The hedgerows hum and buzz with wildlife, there are quaint styles in ageless dry-stone walls, thickets of bramble and blackthorn, meadowsweet and ragwort, and little clumps of trees like sentries against the rolling backdrop of the hills. You can walk for miles, often without seeing another human being. There is a marvellous sense of freedom, and of peace, and you don't have to be a naturalist to appreciate it. It's great training country, too, and I have developed a six-mile circular run which takes me up hill and down dale, a route which is demanding and fulfilling.

Progress, of course, is disconcertingly near. From the patio of our house you can just make out the M62 motorway across the fields, as it drops down from the highest point of the Pennines. M62? Makes you think of a machine-gun, that, and often sounds like one too, if the wind is in the wrong direction. The villagers obviously accept the snarling hum of the traffic; even the cows, sheep and horses graze on unconcernedly as thirty-ton juggernauts stream to and fro interminably, night and day. From our patio window the vehicles look like miniature toys on a conveyor belt, and by now we hardly give the noise or the scene much thought. But there is still the advantage of having a major road link so close, particularly with so many golf clubs in the area – significant now that I have fallen in love with that particular game.

Clifton is six miles due west of Bradford and two from Brighouse, which is just down the hill from the village. When I first went to Yorkshire, I didn't know much about either town, except that Brighouse was the home of one of Britain's most famous brass bands and that Bradford, like Cardiff, was a multicultural city. I remembered, too, that Bradford was the first English town to elect an Asian mayor, and was the home, among others, of former heavyweight boxing champion Richard Dunn, snooker champion Joe Johnson and that controversial headmaster, Ray Honeyford. Then there was that appalling fire at the local football ground, a tragedy which shocked the sporting world and was instrumental in getting the authorities to rethink the standards of safety at sports stadiums.

I learned later that, although both towns were very much Rugby League territory, they also had strong links with Rugby Union, the most important of which was that the Barbarians club was formed in Bradford, on 9 April 1890, at their famous 'oyster supper' at Leuchter's Restaurant in Darley Street. Leuchter's has long gone, having been displaced by Littlewoods department store.

It was much more of a surprise to discover that Brighouse also had a connection with Rugby Union: not only did this old mill town once have a famous rugby club, Brighouse Rangers, formed in 1880, but they used to play my former club, Cardiff, established four years earlier. Cardiff played Brighouse Rangers three times, Cardiff winning and drawing at the Arms Park in 1886 and 1889 but then losing away 0–10 on 6 February 1890. Brighouse eventually played Rugby League, and in 1896–7 topped the Yorkshire Senior League, which included my present club, Bradford Northern. Rangers ceased playing in 1905–6 and, although efforts were made to re-form the club, they eventually disappeared totally from the rugby map.

26

It is fascinating to recall that in those early days Cardiff had fixtures against many other northern clubs, including Bradford, Castleford, Dewsbury, Huddersfield, Leeds, Oldham, Runcorn, Salford, Swinton, Wakefield Trinity and Wigan. It was all to end, of course, with the coming of the 'great divide', when most of the clubs in Lancashire and Yorkshire split from the Rugby Union and formed the Northern Union, which was later to become the Rugby League.

Of understandable interest to me was that one of Cardiff's great players of the past, William 'Buller' Stadden, also had a northern connection, for he moved to Yorkshire in 1886 to play for Dewsbury – before they became a Rugby League club. Buller led the way along which many other Cardiff players, including myself, were to follow. As it happened, he won five of his eight Welsh caps as a Dewsbury player, and is believed to have been the first Welsh international to turn professional – in 1894, when Dewsbury abandoned Rugby Union. Buller played twenty-one times for Yorkshire, but much more significantly he scored the only try of the match which enabled Wales to score their first ever win over England, on 15 February 1890, nine days after Cardiff had lost at Brighouse. The England–Wales match was played, in a manner of speaking, just up the road from Brighouse, at Crown Flatt, Dewsbury – by coincidence Buller's home ground. Apparently there were great mutterings of discontent about the method Buller employed to score his try: he pretended to throw long at a line-out and when the England forwards retreated to cover the gambit, Buller bounced the ball a few feet infield, gathered it himself and sped over for the winning score. 'Cheating,' protested the outraged English. 'Flair,' replied the Welsh. Buller, incidentally, never played for Wales again and it was sixteen years before bouncing the ball in his famed manner was outlawed in Rugby Union, in 1906. On 30 December of the same year, Buller Stadden took his own life. He was forty-six.

Including Bob Ackerman, who is now with Whitehaven, and myself, I learned that twenty-three former Cardiff players who were capped by Wales eventually turned professional. Oddly, I am the only one of those to have moved to Bradford Northern,

27

whose only other capped Welsh players were signed from Swansea (Willie Davies) and Llanelli (Stuart Gallacher and Terry Price). They still talk with glowing admiration in Bradford of Willie Davies's skill, but the Welsh hero of these parts was undoubtedly Trevor Foster, who was never capped by Wales.

'If you end up only half as good as Trevor you'll do OK,' they told me when I first arrived at Odsal. Trevor John French Foster came from a military background, joined Northern as a forward from Newport in 1938, although he also played for Llwynypia, and made three appearances for Cardiff. Like myself, Trevor learned his rugby at a Catholic school – Holy Cross, in Newport – and also found the transition something of a test. Eventually he earned the description of 'the complete footballer' and was to appear in 428 matches for Northern between 1938 and 1955, scoring 128 tries. Trevor loved Yorkshire, too, never returning to his fatherland. Today he is more Yorkshire than Welsh, and he still maintains his Northern connection as a timekeeper with the club. He was one of the first to welcome me to Odsal, and has been a marvellous friend and counsellor ever since. 'A real gentleman,' I was told. I can vouch for it.

4
Prejudice

Soon after I had moved to Yorkshire to begin my Rugby League career, I was followed in the professional game by two other players who had been capped by Wales, Bob Ackerman, with whom I played at Cardiff, and Gary Pearce, who was Llanelli's record points-scorer in 1984–5. Gary's move should have attracted more publicity than it did if only because by signing for Hull he became the 150th Welsh international to have made the leap across the great divide.

That so many capped Welshmen have switched codes is a flattering indication, I suppose, of Rugby League's regard for the quality of players in the Principality. At the same time, 150 (out of the 831 capped by Wales) represents an enormous drain on the playing resources of a very small rugby country, and probably is a mere fraction of the total figure of Welsh converts because many, many players who were never capped also 'went north'.

When I signed for Bradford Northern, my first-class Union career – certainly in international terms – was effectively finished. But most of those capped Welsh players who were beckoned to Rugby League usually did so in their prime, or even before they had fulfilled their potential as Union players. Black armbands were two a penny in a lot of clubs up and down the valleys when a promising player packed his bags and headed north. Depending on how you view it, Wales's loss was Rugby League's gain. Yet this never-ending stream of players leaving Wales since the 1880s perhaps explains the inherent hostility that Rugby League traditionally feels towards the Union game. The poacher is always frowned upon by the gamekeeper.

A good example of this attitude occurred at my former club,

Cardiff. Danny Davies, a former prominent administrator and author of the history of the club (*Cardiff Rugby Club 1876–1975 – History and Statistics*, published 1975), was well known for his aversion to all matters Rugby League. In his book (which is in all respects an excellent and well-researched volume) he admits among other things to being at loggerheads with the Cardiff committee because he 'was not in favour of Rugby League players being admitted into the club-house, even as visitors'. Danny (incidentally the president of the WRU in 1961–2) conceded that the Cardiff committee did not altogether agree with his views. However, he went on to snipe at the fact that ex-Cardiff players Jim Mills, John Bevan and Colin Dixon, with Maurice Richards as reserve, took part in a Rugby League international, 'Wales' (Danny's quotes) v France at Swansea on 16 February 1975. 'These players would have greatly helped Cardiff in 1974–5,' he commented sourly. Although he never indicated that he'd ever watched a Rugby League match, Danny was insistent that as a game it 'lacks variety and is very rough'. To prove this particular point he listed injuries to Dai Watkins (broken arm, broken jaw, broken nose (four times) in his first two years 'up north') and Chico Hopkins (seven black eyes in seven matches), compounding the indictment by declaring that most of the injuries were the result of late and illegal tackles. In a nutshell, Rugby League was a thoroughly ungentlemanly activity and Cardiff should have nothing whatsoever to do with it, or with anyone misguided enough to see his fortune on northern fields. As someone who has now experienced both codes, I can safely say that Danny's judgements were a trifle skew-whiff on all counts.

It must have been disconcerting for Danny to have discovered, during his researches into Cardiff's early history, that Buller Stadden, one of the club's stalwarts of those days, not only went north, but became the first Welsh international to play Rugby League.

There are signs, however, that prejudice against Rugby League, and much of the deep-rooted and bitter enmity that existed between the codes, is on the wane, and I for one am very glad of it. I thought this before I signed for Northern, although naturally my views have since hardened in this respect. The unfortunate affair concerning the young Cardiff wing, Steve Ford, banned by the WRU in 1986 for taking part in a Rugby League trial, is evidence that the wrath of authority can, and most certainly will, fall on hapless heads; and I'm sure that regardless of changing attitudes there will always be plenty of die-hards in Union who will go to their graves convinced of the evils of professional rugby.

But when, for instance, Dai Watkins can be invited as a guest speaker at his former Rugby Union club's dinner in Newport, as he was in 1986, you begin to believe that tolerance has given bigotry a good hand-off. And when you witness the fundamental changes that are occurring at the highest level in Rugby Union, at the International Board with regard to broken-time pay-ments, for instance, one is entitled to think that perhaps many of today's administrators are no longer hostage to principles of a bygone age.

They tell me that Dai cuts an impressive figure when he is given the chance to make an after-dinner speech. I'm pretty sure that his ability in this respect outweighed any moral indignation of certain members of the Newport club about his having left them to become a Rugby League player. Indeed, there may be a pattern emerging with regard to the kind of people Rugby Union clubs invite to their dinners. Early in 1986 I received the following letter, c/o Bradford Northern:

Dear Mr Holmes,

In view of you now having moved to Yorkshire from Cardiff, my Committee has asked me to write to you to determine if you would be available to speak at our Annual Dinner which is to be held on Friday 9th May 1986 in Halifax.

I hope that you are available, and on your favourable response I can furnish you with more details.

Hoping for a positive reply . . .

The invitation came from the Heath Rugby Union Club in West Yorkshire. Sadly, and unlike Dai Watkins, I was unable to accept, for at the time I was recovering from injury and had yet to move to a new home in Yorkshire.

Gary Pearce also broke new ground in 1986. In October, at one of Welsh rugby's top social events of the year at the Cardiff Crest Hotel, Gary presented my old Cardiff pal, Adrian Hadley, with the Lloyd Lewis Memorial Trophy as man-of-the-match in the Schweppes Welsh Cup Final. Nothing special in that, you might suppose, except that Gary was the first player who had turned Rugby League to be invited to make the presentation. Traditionally the presentation is made by the previous year's winner, and it fell upon Gary, awarded the Trophy in 1985, to carry on the convention, even though meanwhile he had committed the unspeakable in some people's eyes by deciding to play for pay. The Welsh Rugby Writers' Association, organisers of the event, had voted Adrian man-of-the-match for scoring three tries against Newport in the 1986 Cup Final and, from what I gather, that body had no qualms whatsoever in inviting Gary back from Hull to perform a duty which in times gone by would have been unthinkable.

Hull's attitude to the occasion was interesting. The club chairman, Peter Darley, enthusiastically supported Gary's attendance and rearranged Hull's training schedules so that he could travel to Cardiff. Hull not only gave Gary their benevolence and blessing, but viewed his participation not so much as any kind of reflected glory but as a genuine wish to foster a bond between the two codes. Being of a mildly suspicious nature, only one question persists – I wonder who paid Gary's expenses, Hull or the Welsh rugby scribes?

Another concrete example of changing attitudes was the visit of Bath's coaching staff to Hull Kingston Rovers in 1985. It caused a stir, to say the least, when representatives from one of England's premier Rugby Union clubs decided that a Rugby League club's training and coaching methods were worthy of first-hand examination. They sought Hull KR's help, and got it. Jack Rowell, Bath's coach, and his assistants, Dave Robson and Tom Hudson, spent two days on Humberside, with Hull KR coach, Roger Millward, as their host.

Since I was by then something of an old hand up north, I was in no way surprised that Hull KR should have welcomed their amateur brethren warmly and openly, and afforded them access to training sessions, as well as allowing frank discussions with individual players.

Bath regarded the trip as tremendously successful and they declared to a man that they had learned a great deal from Hull KR's methods in improving skills, training and fitness, much of which they were sure would benefit their own club. One visit of this nature, of course, does not mean that other Rugby Union clubs will follow suit. Nevertheless, it is a significant beginning, which perhaps may lead to further co-operation between the two codes. That is something which many in both sports will welcome. And the way Bath played in 1986, defeating many of the best clubs in the land – including all the top clubs in Wales – suggests they might already have adopted some League technique, and benefited from it in real terms.

My own experience also suggests that things ain't what they used to be. When I informed Cardiff of my intention to join Bradford Northern, Alun Priday, the Cardiff secretary, wrote me a formal letter, thanking me for my services and expressing the good wishes of the club and its committee for success in my new career. Any time that I wanted to visit the club, the letter went on, I would be made very welcome – a suggestion, no doubt, that might have made dear old Danny Davies turn somersaults in his grave. Incidentally, I was a pall-bearer at Danny's funeral. I knew him well, as a great servant and friend of Cardiff.

It goes without saying that I enormously appreciated that letter from Alun Priday; I'd like to think of it as more than a goodwill gesture for it was marvellously reassuring that Cardiff – my club and my life for so many years – were not going to reject me as a pariah simply because I had decided to pursue another job, which is how I regard my career in Rugby League. Really, I ought not to have been so surprised and flattered. The gesture is typical of the mature and magnanimous attitude that prevails there and is among the reasons they remain one of the world's great Union clubs.

I have not yet had the opportunity to take up Cardiff's invitation, but presumably the promise and sentiment are unchanged: friends who regularly visit the Arms Park tell me

MY LIFE IN RUGBY

that my portrait, unadorned by any anti-Rugby League graffiti, still hangs in the members' bar. As long as the picture's there, I imagine it's unlikely there will be a brawny steward at the entrance with orders to prevent my popping in for a pint of Brain's. It all adds to the growing evidence that the differences which kept the two sports apart have been eroded. That must be a good thing, and is an end to which I personally will devote much effort, for I love and respect both games.

That portrait, incidentally, has an interesting history. It was presented to the club just before Cardiff kicked off against Bridgend at the Arms Park in November 1984. Stan Bowes, Cardiff's chairman, was appointed to accept it formally, the handing-over ceremony taking place in front of the main stand before the two teams took the field. Alun Priday, the MC, explained the proceedings to the crowd with due solemnity, and the portrait was duly handed over for safe custody to Stan, who was standing near the gate through which the players run on to the field. Stan was holding the picture in both hands and acknowledging the crowd's applause when, on cue, Bridgend's players ran out, led by their captain, Gareth 'Sam' Williams. Now, either Stan was too close to the players' gate or Sam – intent on making a grand entrance – didn't see him, until it was too late. Sam had a fair head of steam on, but at the last moment he attempted an adroit side-step to avoid the Cardiff chairman, who's a pretty burly guy. Apparently Stan didn't make too much of an effort to get out of the way. Be that as it may, Sam's side-step, with due respect, has never been in the Gerald Davies class, and on this occasion it was not adroit enough. As he raced out on to the park, a collision was inevitable, his knee coming into sharp contact with the picture that Stan was still holding in front of him, the glass shattering with a resounding crash. Stan reared back as if someone had thrown a stun grenade at him. The Bridgend captain meanwhile continued his run with the rest of his team trooping behind him, and it was clear for a moment or two during their warm-up passing that none of them, Sam included, had an inkling that an extraordinary accident had taken place. The Cardiff team followed them out almost immediately, and only when he felt a twinge of pain and saw

34

blood flowing down his leg, did Sam realise he had been injured. So serious, in fact, was the gash that he had to ask the referee's permission to leave the field before kick-off so that he could be treated. Six stitches were put in the cut and, as if that were not bad enough, Sam was no longer fit to go back on, so that Bridgend had to field a substitute before the match had even started. Thus, uniquely, Sam became the only visiting captain ever to lead a side out on to the Arms Park and not take part in a match. To say he was disgruntled about the whole incident is an understatement. Nor did it help that Bridgend, without their captain, thereupon contrived to lose the match as well. Naturally, Stan the saboteur came in for a lot of ribbing from Bridgend and some of the Cardiff committee. I suppose I can count myself lucky I didn't get the blame – after all, it was a picture of me.

This is not to suggest that all prejudice against Rugby League has disappeared. I'm reminded of that by an amusing incident which occurred during a return visit to Wales early in 1986, when I went to watch, as a casual observer, a semi-final at Ceidelyn Park of the Ninian Stuart Cup, one of the many Rugby Union competitions that annually take place in and around Cardiff. It was a good opportunity to take my Labrador, Shar, for her daily constitutional. Shar is one of those dogs who rarely leaves your side. Other dogs – and strangers – she regards, in her shy, retiring way, as enemies. Confident that she'd lie obediently close as I watched the match, I let her off her lead. Not for the first time in our association, Shar proved me wrong. Before I realised it, she had quit her dutiful perambulations around my legs, and suddenly appeared in the middle of the pitch doing something she shouldn't have been doing – not there anyway. The game was abruptly stopped, and the players were obviously appalled at this breach of etiquette. Many a dog-owner's fatherhood was immediately called into question, but this particular one clearly had to react rapidly to the fraught situation by proving that a single curt command could bring the prodigal instantly back from the scene of the crime and allow the lads to continue their game.

'Here, Shar, back here,' I called from the touch-line. 'Come here NOW!' My summons gave way to shouts of desperation. Predictably, Shar ignored all my calls. She was thoroughly enjoying herself, jinking and side-stepping with glee as the players tried fruitlessly to nab her. Alas, one of them, Rumney's full-back, didn't seem to have any sense of humour, nor did he take kindly to Shar's playful jump on to his back. He gave her a cuff, the devil. Insult the owner, by all means, but don't maltreat his best friend, I muttered darkly as, at last, I realised that I had to leave the relative obscurity of the touch-line and go on to the field to collect the miscreant.

I suppose, by strict interpretation of Rugby Union laws, my very act of stepping on to a pitch during a match was enough to have professionalised every player on the field. Not surprisingly, I was immediately recognised. 'Get *him* off the pitch,' a wag in the crowd shouted. 'He can't play, he's a professional!' No one need have worried. I wasn't exactly kitted to be the first Rugby League player to take an impromptu part in an amateur Rugby Union match in Wales. I was wearing green wellies, flat hat and farmer's jacket. My Yorkshire outfit, you might say.

On reflection, and after a couple of years in Rugby League, I can't help but ask myself: 'Why should there be any prejudice?'

It's 1987 and a lot of things have changed, but the basic truth is that apart from the posts and the shape of the ball Rugby League and Rugby Union could not be more different. They are completely different games.

For the foreseeable future, League will be essentially a northern game and the professional code will be confined to its present stronghold. The game offers absolutely no real threat to Rugby Union, or vice versa. Now that amateur Rugby League has been accepted by the Union authorities, which allows players to take part in either code without prejudice, why not take this advance a step further? I think it would be a good idea – from everybody's point of view – if, for instance, a Union player were allowed, say, two or three 'trial' matches at Rugby League before he came to a decision. Obviously, that player would not be paid. If he liked League he could then decide to take it up; if not he could return to the Union fold without discredit. As it is, he is more likely to be caught up in no man's land, or no play land, like poor Steve Ford who has played no rugby at all for two years because the Union game ruled against his return.

Both are great games, with obvious attractions for the players. But they should be big enough to help each other with the ultimate aim of improving the standards of rugby itself throughout Britain. Have your rules by all means but don't let them strangle either game.

5

Born

On 9 March 1957 Wales beat Ireland at Cardiff thanks to two penalty goals by Terry Davies. As I was born the next day, a few minutes' walk from the scene of the Llanelli full-back's triumph, I have sometimes toyed with the notion that my parents named me Terence David as their way of acknowledging the hero of that chill, dank afternoon at the Arms Park.

Alas, little could be more fanciful or further from reality. Like all good Catholic parents, they had already decided on the names they wanted if their third child was a boy. Moreover, despite the proximity of my birthplace at 74 Churchill Way to the shrine of Welsh rugby, neither of my parents was sufficiently enamoured of the game at that time even to consider linking the newest addition to the Holmes household with a rugby player, hero or not. More likely, had they been the fans they were later to become, Terence David would likely have given way to Terence John, the given names of Wales's match-winner that day, from Llwynhendy.

No doubt my parents had other, more pressing matters on their minds when I came into this world. Life at the time was very tough for them, as it was for all the working folk who lived in Churchill Way.

The only advantage in having been born so close to one of the world's great rugby arenas was that I didn't have to walk very far to see a match. I'd have to go a bit, though, to cap Okey Geffin, the Springbok prop who was born a hundred yards or so from Ellis Park, the cathedral of South African rugby, in Johannesburg. Maybe his parents should have called him Ellis Geffin – he was registered without a given name and adopted Aaron Okey later in life.

The house in which I was born was also my mother's birth-place, although when my grandfather first moved there it was known as 13 East Terrace. Sadly, although it was only a humble terraced abode, it is no longer there, reduced to rubble by the bulldozers in the name of progress. In 1968, the street was condemned as unfit for human habitation and flattened. My parents were rehoused in Fairwater council estate a few miles away, and the reason they were given for being uprooted was that the levelling of Churchill Way was part of a vast urban redevelopment, which entailed moving every resident away from the city centre. It was redeveloped all right. They made it into a car park. It still is.

I was ten years old, and I remember that move only because it was the first major upheaval of my life. My recollections of Churchill Way are few and vague. Had the street been in another city, in another part of the country, it might not have lasted even as long as it did. The thirty or so terraced houses were built in the 1880s and like so many so-called homes of that time they were erected with scant attention to the practical needs of the working-class folk who had to live in them. Although three up and two down, there was no bathroom, no hot water even, and the loo was outside in a small back yard. It was a primitive existence at best for the men and women who lived and worked in a city which in its prime was one of the major ports in the world. The days are long gone, however, since Cardiff was the greatest coal-exporting port of the industrial world.

Most of Cardiff's labour force during the years either side of the turn of the century came from other parts of the British Isles – England, Scotland and Ireland – although with the influx of many other nationalities, black and white, it became one of the first multicultural cities in the country. Even today, with the docks idle and many factories closed down, you will hear the unmistakable throaty Cardiff accent on the lips of West Indians, Chinese, Muslims and Jews. All of them call Cardiff home. Most of them regard themselves unreservedly as Welsh, as I do, although by ancestry and culture we were Irish, on both sides of the family. My mother and father, however, were both born and bred in Cardiff and their links with the 'old country' were long severed by the time I came into the world. They never regarded themselves as other than Welsh because they were born in Wales and reared in Welsh culture – or, rather, Cardiff culture, which is something different altogether.

No matter what your original strain or creed, born in Cardiff meant you were a Cardiffian always. Being a Welshman as well was a bonus, and I grew up in a relatively carefree cosmopolitan society in which religious prejudice and racialism were unknown.

With my Irish connections it was obvious that I would be brought up as a Catholic. That was as much the consequence of living in an area in which the Irish outnumbered all other nationalities as of any particular desire by my parents to bring me up in the Catholic faith. It is incredible to think that at one time there was believed to be as many as 20,000 Irishmen in Glamorgan alone, most of whom had been imported as cheap labour by the chief architect of both the splendour and the poverty of Cardiff, the Marquis of Bute. The Marquis became one of Britain's richest men, largely because of his ownership of the coal mines up the valleys. Generally unloved, he was criticised for being a harsh, unrelenting taskmaster of his workforce, who kept wages down and ignored the plight of the poor. At the same time, he was largely influential in the establishment of Cardiff as a great trading port as well as in the building of many of the city's superb civic buildings and parks. In a way, the fact that Cardiff Arms Park is now the WRU headquarters is largely due to him, for the national stadium complex is built on land formerly owned by him and sold as fields and reclaimed land in the 1920s.

Naturally enough, the role of the Marquis of Bute in the development of Cardiff was part of the local history I was required to learn at school. The fact that he was a Catholic, too, ensured his place on the curriculum. I am still not sure whether I was supposed to regard him as benefactor or ogre. Either way, the Cardiff I grew up in and came to know and love was a Cardiff which he had created.

Hitler did his best to change the appearance of Cardiff during the Second World War. My mother vividly recalls the bombs whistling down, although she barely remembers the day when during one attack my grandfather had to have his leg amputated after receiving a shrapnel wound. Grandfather – who was named Gwilym Driscoll – was a real character, full of the dry humour and chat that personify Cardiff. I was very fond of him, and as a boy I used to help him out as he click-clacked around the city streets on crutches, pushing his fruit and vegetables barrow. With my father out at work, usually down the docks, I saw much more of Gwilym and was probably more influenced by him than by anyone else. I missed him badly when he died.

I see a lot of Grandfather in my mother. Phyllis (I've always called her that, never 'Mother') has no airs or graces. She's down to earth and independent, and proud of it. She's also a fusspot, a bit of a Hilda Ogden, refusing to keep still, always finding something to do. Even when she comes visiting, she doesn't sit and relax; if she hasn't got the Hoover out, or the dustpan and brush, she isn't happy. She's funny too. She smokes, knowing I find it distasteful, so when she wants a drag she'll make some excuse to go into another room or out into the garden. I tell her I don't mind, but she takes no notice. It's a sort of game between us.

I keep telling her that it is about time that she started to take things easier. All her life she has worked very hard. For many years she laboured at two jobs, cleaning other people's houses and working down at the docks, usually bagging potatoes, which is a pretty miserable, back-breaking task. It was something of an irony – recalling the role of the potato in Irish history – that a lot of the spuds Phyllis and other women of Irish stock helped unload down in West Dock came from Ireland. The 'Potato Women' laboured long and hard and complained little, and Phyllis was always talking of the special camaraderie that existed in what was essentially a man's world, and a tough one at that. She did it, she says, to give her children a chance in life which she never had. She doesn't go around boasting about it, but she's very proud that my two older sisters did well academically, Christine becoming a graduate of Sheffield University and Catherine, after college in Southampton, getting a good job in the civil service. Even though both left home to get married,

Phyllis sees them as often as possible. That's easy as far as Catherine is concerned. She lives in Barry, just down the road from Cardiff, with her husband Bob and children James, Sian-Marie and Luke. Christine, though, ventured farther afield. She married Carlo, an Italian tennis coach, and she lives with him in Florence with their two children, Sean and Dylan. Phyllis isn't one for travelling, but she regularly flies out to Florence just to 'keep in touch' with the Italian branch of the family. 'Still,' she says, 'I can't wait to get back to Cardiff.' A bit like me, I suppose.

Even though I was to prove the non-academic member of the family, I have a sneaking feeling that Phyllis was more pleased by the way things turned out for me than they did for Christine and Catherine. As mother and son we were always very close, and although she ceaselessly trumpeted on to all three of us about the need for getting qualifications, she didn't bat an eyelid when I showed more interest in sport than in schoolwork. It was she, in fact, who sustained my sporting activities far more than my father did. She didn't push me exactly, but she was always there, supportive and encouraging. It helped to establish a strong and close bond between us, and I was often surprised at how much she knew about sport, particularly rugby.

Phyllis worked hard to provide her share for the Holmes household, but even so there was never very much of it. Luxuries were non-existent, although I can't really say we ever went without, in basic living terms. It was not until much later in life that I appreciated how much she'd done for me, how she had scrimped and saved so that I could have a new pair of boots, a tracksuit or travelling money.

Apart from Susan, my wife, and a few close friends, I usually turned to my mother for counsel. After my father died, if ever I was undecided about something really important, I'd go to her. We'd chat and pick the bones. It seemed a perfectly natural thing to do, although sometimes I knew I wouldn't heed her advice. When I was considering Bradford Northern's offer to turn professional, once again I sought her opinion. I knew she'd be very much against my leaving Cardiff, even though she realised that the financial side of the deal would set Susan and me up for life.

'No, don't go,' she said. 'It sounds like a lot of money, but it's not worth it. What if you go up there and get injured or something?'

Looking back, that seemed to confirm what I'd always feared. Phyllis had a sixth sense and, sure enough, in my first match for Bradford her foreboding was confirmed.

After that injury, there was a lot of speculation and comment in the Press. It varied from good objective criticism to something bordering on libel. Undoubtedly, the nastiest, most malicious comments appeared in the *Sun*, the gist being that I was neither fit enough nor good enough to be a Rugby League player. Being a phlegmatic sort of bloke, a bit thick-skinned you might say, this pompous tirade didn't bother me much – and that's the truth. The article didn't make me happy, but at the same time it wasn't going to ruin my day. However, many of my friends, particularly back in Wales, were quick to let me know of their sense of outrage. To say that my mother was bitterly upset about it was an understatement.

Phyllis took the *Sun* regularly and on the day the article appeared she was on tenterhooks because she needed only two more numbers to hit the jackpot in their Bingo game. When she read the article, she rang me. 'Have you read the *Sun*?' she asked. 'It's terrible, those awful things they've said about you. I'm never going to buy that paper again.' I tried to tell her not to worry about it; nobody believed anything the *Sun* said, anyway. 'I don't care,' she replied. 'If people can write that sort of thing, there's only one thing you've got to do. Give Bradford their money back and come home!'

I realised she was going to take a lot of persuading to change her mind. 'Come on, Phyllis, if you get those last two Bingo numbers and you win, are you going to give them the money back?' She thought about it for a moment. 'Yes, you're right. I'll keep on taking the paper. If I get those two numbers I'll take the money – then I'll stop buying the paper. That'll teach 'em, won't it?'

Needless to say, Phyllis didn't get her two numbers. And she still buys the *Sun*, which is OK by me because I think they've stopped having a go at me now.

My father, whom I always addressed as Dai, was born at Sandon Place, in Adamstown, opposite Cardiff Gaol. As with my mother, few things came easy for him in a working career which embraced many varied jobs, although I think his greatest satisfaction came from his time as a seaman, working out of Cardiff Docks. I don't suppose that at any period of his life he had any real money. His pleasures were few, too. His fun was almost entirely confined to drinking in local pubs with his pals and waxing on about the good old days they had known at sea and on the docks.

He had a lot of interests, but sport, including rugby, was hardly his abiding passion. The fact that his son was totally wrapped up in sport was rarely a subject of conversation. This was understandable. He was far too busy earning a living in a tough environment, in which if you had a job you made sure you kept it. He'd ask me occasionally how I'd got on, or where I was playing next week, but he never indicated that he was really interested. It's possible that he found all forms of sport dull. Phyllis, of course, more than made up for that. As it happens, it didn't bother me that my father didn't do handstands when I began to play regularly for Cardiff and then Wales. In fact, he never even came to see me play until I was about twenty-three. He soon established a rapport with other Cardiff fans, but again the rugby really didn't get to him. Most times he'd stand and watch only until half-time, and then he'd make his way to the bar. That's where the fun was as far as Dai Holmes was concerned. By the time the match had finished, and I'd joined him there after showering and changing, he was merry, to say the least, semi-incoherent on his favourite tipples, black rum and Brain's Bitter. I could always guess from a distance just how far over the top he'd gone when he'd announce his favourite party piece: 'I've got a Welsh cap, too, you know. For drinking.' 'Time to go home, Dai,' I'd say to him gently. I didn't really mind his après-match sessions in the club. He was having fun, and I'm the last bloke in the world who'd think of stopping him.

Dai, then, had a pretty detached view of sport. Team pictures, my Welsh cap, and the odd trophy or two were just 'things' to him. I didn't appreciate his indifference until one day, when I was walking home from work, I spotted him cycling up the road – wearing my Welsh blazer. I made a mild, smiling protest, suggesting it was not the done thing. Only the owner was entitled to wear a Welsh blazer. 'Don't go on, boy,' he retorted. 'It's only a bloody jacket!' He couldn't have cared less, of course. I should have known better, because he always had a funny idea about clothes. Once I gave him a pair of black patent-leather shoes, although I knew we took different sizes. Obviously they didn't fit. Dai solved the problem with his usual panache. He cut out the heels, and promptly set off to the pub wearing them. 'They were a bit tight,' he explained.

My father died of cancer. He suffered from this most awful of diseases for years, but it was typical of him that he never talked much to anyone, even his family, about 'his problem'. I can't ever remember him complaining, or bemoaning his fate, even near the end when he was in dreadful pain. Never once did he speak of the agony. He didn't have to. You could see it in his eyes. If anything has left an indelible mark on me, it was those last few days of my father's life, watching the tragic drama of a once robust and active man slowly, insidiously, wasting away. I'd have done anything, anything at all, to help him and alleviate his suffering. But I felt so helpless. Useless. The end, when it came, was as much a relief for the family as it was for him.

I was twenty-five when he died, on 1 February 1982. He was sixty-three. A requiem mass was held at St David's Cathedral, in Charles Street, which was 300 yards from the site of our old house in Churchill Way. We placed him in his last resting place at Western Cemetery in the Cowbridge Road. It was an awful day, the cold biting into your bones, and the rain coming down in buckets. Typical Cardiff funeral, too. They came in their hundreds, a lot of his old pals and work-mates, dockers, seamen and labourers, as well as friends and acquaintances of mine, folk like Gareth Davies, Jeff Squire, John Dawes, Stan Bowes and John Ryan, and others, many others, faces in the crowd. There were so many, I couldn't remember them all, just a sea of faces, some seeking me out with their eyes and nodding understandingly,

45

others squeezing my hand or embracing me. Hardly a word was said. It wasn't necessary. Their presence was enough, reassurance in a silent homage. They came to pay their last respects in their own private way, and then for most of them it was off to the pub where they lifted their glasses and reminisced and said what a great bloke Dai Holmes was. By the end of the night, no doubt, when the Brain's Bitter and the Guinness had reached parts that no lager would reach, it was: 'That b——, he owed me five quid.' As I said, a typical Cardiff funeral.

Afterwards, I took my mother home, and couldn't believe how brave she'd been. At the graveside she had looked so small, fragile and helpless. Yet she was still defying the world in her way, and had given all the outward appearance of control, bravely and stoically accepting an event which tears great holes in the fabric of family life. She never broke down once. I did. I cried.

Later that night, for the first time since he had died, I found myself thinking about my father and the hard life he had led; and now, too late, I reproached myself that I'd not got to know him better. We were close, buddies in a way, but I didn't really know him. Like a lot of kids, I'd taken him for granted. It never occurred to me that one day he wouldn't be there when I got home. Why hadn't I asked him all those questions about his life, his thoughts, his hopes and ambitions? Pondering fate, I felt guilty, and so empty, for suddenly the fact that he was no longer there seemed to show up how selfish I was, thinking only about my own life and my own future. So many questions, all unanswered. And now he was gone.

At the time, I had to face up to other questions of conscience. I was due to play for Wales against France at the Arms Park five days after he died, and I was quite at a loss what to do. All those connected with the Welsh team were tremendous, very supportive and understanding. Rhys Williams, the chairman of the selectors, told me: 'You do what you think you should do. If you think you shouldn't play, we'll understand. I'll leave it to you.'

I had withdrawn from the squad session on the Monday but I was far from certain whether I should withdraw from the team as well. It was one of the most difficult decisions of my life. On the

46

one hand I acknowledged that it might be considered disrespect-
ful, even uncaring, if I played. On the other I kept reassuring
myself that my father was one of those who had spent his life
insisting, come what may, that life must go on. I told myself that
he would have wanted me to play. In the end, that knowledge
tipped the balance. Two days before the match I rang Rhys. 'I'll
play,' I told him. I didn't add that by now I had steeled myself to
go out against France and play the game of my life . . . for my
father, as a final tribute to him.

It turned out to be Wales's only victory of the season. Our
forwards had a good day and, although our midfield stuttered a
bit, we were always too sharp for the French. David Burnett, the
Irish referee who'd sent off Paul Ringer at Twickenham the
previous season, tolerated little and penalised a lot. Poor France
didn't know whether they were coming or going, and Gwyn
Evans equalled the world record with six penalty goals. Steve
Sutton, I remember, had a very good match on his début in the
middle of the line-out, and Jeff Squire and Clive Burgess, the
brains and brawn of our back row, made my job a lot easier.
Give the French their due, though, they tackled like fiends and
there were times when I suspected we might be winning the
match on penalties alone. But I had a promise to keep.

Squire set up the chance by putting Ray Gravell away on a
typical rumbustious midfield sortie. A deft inside pass from
Gravs to Bob Ackerman created a small but important space out
on the wing and Bob made further distance, sensing all the time
that I was coming up in support. I took his pass and went like a
bullock for the line. No finesse. Just brute strength. A couple of
Frenchmen came at me and hit me, but nothing, I'd decided by
then, was going to stop me. I crashed over wide out, with the
tacklers clinging like leeches. It was Wales's only try that day.
'That one's for you, Dai,' I told myself. I've scored more
spectacular tries for Wales, but the memory of that one against
France will stay with me as long as the River Taff winds its way
past the Arms Park.

Another of my stamping grounds, and only just down the road
from where I was born, is Butetown, better known as Tiger Bay.

This, more than any other part of the city, epitomises the multinational mix of Cardiff, a crucible of numerous races, creeds and colours who have made the city their home over the years. Although the march of time has eroded some of the character of the place, with the closure of the docks and other works forcing the inhabitants to uproot and depart with kith, kin and chattels, in many ways it is still the heartbeat of the city. Even as for-sale signs mushroom on factory and shop, and the housing stock is knocked down and replenished, Tiger Bay still roars its defiance at bulldozer and crane; some inhabitants, born and bred there, are determined to stay, to live and to die in a place they've made their home. Others, like Shirley Bassey, who have moved on, still remember it with affection and pride. 'Where do you come from?' Shirley was once asked. 'Tiger Bay,' she answered. Not Cardiff, mark you. But T-I-G-E-R B-A-Y. Once I had a lot of friends there, and was a frequent visitor to café, restaurant, club and pub. It wasn't chic or elegant or smart but, shabby or not, here was a flourishing and friendly community in which everyone seemed to wear a welcome on his sleeve. When I go back now, I am struck by the changes, by the upheavals and the decline. But I'm sure the heritage will live on.

One of the most interesting facts about Butetown is that it's an area which has produced not only many a fine footballer, Rugby Union player, boxer and pop star, but also two of the greatest Rugby League players of all time, Gus Risman and Billy Boston. Both were pupils at the same school in South Church Street. By curious quirk, neither of these prodigiously talented players was ever capped by Wales at Rugby Union, although Risman's son, Bev, who was born in Salford, played eight times for England and was a British Lion of 1959.

Like myself, Billy Boston possessed more than a dram or two of Irish blood in his veins – his mother was Cardiff–Irish, and his father was of West Indian stock: that good old Tiger Bay nationality mix, once again. At different times we both played for Wales Youth and Cardiff District. Billy also played for CIACs, the docklands club which gave many a local youngster his first taste of organised sport. I never played for them but the

CIACs were – and still are – a wonderful club, one of the best in Cardiff and District rugby. My fate was determined because, without enticing alternatives, I moved on from Cardiff Youth through to the first XV; Billy's destiny, fame and fortune had been decided at the age of eighteen by call-up for National Service, which took him away from Butetown and Cardiff and Wales – forever. He signed for Wigan whilst serving in England with the Royal Signals in 1953.

Even as a schoolboy in a rugby-mad country, Billy Boston was a living legend to my generation. In a gossip-shop like Cardiff you couldn't help knowing what was happening in the world of sport. Pythagoras and declensions didn't matter; you breathed in sporting facts like the air. When Cardiff folk were not talking in pub, street and market place about, say, their adopted son and celebrity of the day, Cliff Morgan, their daily chat centred on the deeds of another hero, a prodigal who had gone, but who was performing wondrous deeds 'up north'. You just cocked your ear and you knew it all. Billy Boston was literally a household name.

I never saw Billy play. I was only eleven when he retired, in 1968, after sixteen seasons and a phenomenal 571 tries in Rugby League. From all accounts, and folklore, Cardiff town would have been proud of him, would have taken him to their hearts as one of their own: but for fate he would certainly have worn the blue and black of Cardiff RFC and the scarlet of Wales. Robert Gate, in his book *Gone North*, hinted at the great talent lost to Welsh rugby at such a young age when he wrote:

When Welsh Rugby Union folk get together and talk of great wingers they will discuss Willie Llewellyn, Teddy Morgan, Johnny Williams, Rowe Harding, Ken Jones, Dewi Bebb, Stuart Watkins, Gerald Davies and J. J. Williams. They may even recall those who went north such as Johnny Ring, Frank Evans, Jack Morley, Arthur Bassett, Maurice Richards and John Bevan.

It would surprise them to know that Rugby League folk would swear that if all the best qualities of those fine players could be invested in one player, then that player might just about be good enough to have under-studied Bouncing Bill Boston.

Billy's popularity and fame in Rugby League have withstood the test of time. There are some who say he was the best ever. I'll wager that, had I told everyone 'up north' that I came from the same place as Billy Boston, my value as a player might well have doubled at a stroke, and I'd be forever basking in reflected glory. At worst, I'd have been bought drinks all night by mere mention of the fact.

Gus Risman, too, must have been a very good player. He played seventeen times for Great Britain between 1932 and 1946. The only Welshmen to have played more often were Boston, Tommy Harris of Hull, and Wigan's Jim Sullivan. None of these, though, matched Gus's fourteen years as a Test player, a record span in Rugby League. His qualities of leadership, too, were time-resistant. He captained Great Britain three times in 1936 and ten years later he came back to skipper the British tour to Australia and New Zealand.

6

Work

As I left school at sixteen with two 'O' levels and six CSEs, my job prospects were understandably limited. I had no experience, no qualifications and I quickly realised that if I was to make a mark in life, I was going to need a lot of luck.

As a child, from the age of four or five, I used to accompany my mother when she worked on a fruit and veg barrow with my grandfather, Gwilym, and his sons, Vincent and Tony, usually in a little lane off Queen's Street, behind Marks & Spencer and the Taff Vale pub, now demolished. It used to be a folksy thoroughfare in which people would stop and barter with the vendors, chatting and gossiping all the time, an animated, villagey community which was as much part of the Cardiff scene as Brain's Dark. The barrow, which also carried toys and gifts of all kinds, toured the whole central area of the city, with me in tow. I suppose this is when I first started to appreciate and understand Cardiff and Cardiff folk. I became streetwise in every sense of the word, following Gwilym around, marvelling at the verbal cut-and-thrust and the humour.

There was excitement, too, sometimes a run and chase when the local bobbies made an appearance. In those days everyone was supposed to have a street trader's licence. The police nicked Gwilym every now and then and he paid the fine without protest. It was a sort of game. There was no malice, and few comebacks. It would have been easier to have got the licence. He never did. Probably it would have spoiled it all for him, his little game in the streets, the arcades and the maze of quiet, hidden alleyways that made up the centre of the city, and which he loved. By the time I left school I knew them intimately and loved them, too, familiar with every nook and cranny, and all the characters who lived and

51

worked there. I learned many things in the streets, except perhaps any practical skills which would have helped me find a job and keep it.

Aware of my lack of qualifications, I took up a couple of apprenticeships after leaving school. I never got far. Both companies went bust – not, I hasten to add, because of anything I did or didn't do. By this time I had met Sue, and through her I renewed an earlier association with her sister Ursula's future husband, Tommy Foley. With Sue and myself going steady, I was fostered almost as part of the family, and Tommy announced one day that he had found me a job with his father – yet another Tommy – in a company called Tee-Jay Contractors. I was literally on the scrap heap by the time I was seventeen. My life was about to change dramatically. Suddenly I had a job, and security, and with it came an unaccustomed confidence to face the world.

For a lot of people, being a scrap man probably conjures up a picture of a flea-bitten horse pulling a run-down cart through the back-streets, with shady Steptoe & Son characters eager to fiddle unsuspecting old ladies out of their brass candlesticks and then flogging them to a dealer or antique shop at a colossal profit.

My life in scrap, I'm happy to say, was rather less disreputable, and certainly not as fanciful. I worked for a scrap company with a big turnover and staff. Strictly legit, all contracts and PAYE. Our job consisted largely of demolishing disused factories and warehouses, clearing the rubble and disposing of the various metal elements to firms that specialised in reprocessing. It's interesting to contemplate that some piece of steel I hacked out of a dockside warehouse could now be a razor-blade or a safety-pin.

It was a darned sight harder work, too, than Steptoe's casual trading, for often you found yourself facing indestructible mountains of brick and stone, massive girders and towering steel or concrete stanchions. No horse-and-cart for these; more likely bulldozer, JCB, crane and thirty-ton HGVs. A scrapman is a jack-of-all-trades, really, accumulating the skills and experience of the tradesmen who constructed the building in the first place, and in many cases, I can tell you, they built them to last. One moment you're a steeplejack, the next a burner, plate-layer or concreter. It was handy to know how our ancestral craftsmen performed their particular job for it could help when you had to dismantle the products of their skill, sweat and labour.

At the time, I thought of it merely as a job – 'on the scrap', as we called it. It was just a means to an end, something which brought me in a pay-packet at the end of the week, and enabled me to dabble in life's pleasures, particularly sport, which totally preoccupied my non-working hours.

Looking back, maybe I didn't fully appreciate that those were very important years and how the job helped to mould my character and attitude. It never occurred to me, either, that the work I was involved in was tough and dangerous, that there was an easier way of making a crust. I enjoyed it, for there were a lot of great characters in the trade, some of whom became friends for life, folk who respected you not because you were a good rugby player but because you were as capable as they were in highly demanding work.

I suppose some may spurn the role of the scrapman in society or regard his job as a music-hall joke. In my view, the scrap trade is a physically testing occupation which cultivates self-esteem, pride and commitment to a job well done, and which develops feelings of mutual trust and loyalty. That may sound high-flown, but I believe these are qualities which make for lasting friend-ships. Now that I have moved on, as it were, to a different life and job, I can still look back to my days on the scrap with affection. It was hard, but it was also fun. A bit like rugby, I suppose.

I can understand some people raising their hands in horror at the idea that I spent part of my life flattening some of the relics of our industrial past. The preservationists have a case, but there are other viewpoints, just as valid. It should be remembered that not all time-worn industrial or commercial buildings can be regarded as having aesthetic appeal or worthy of saving for posterity. Some, I agree, should be protected, as an example of the skill and craftsmanship of yesterday's industrial architects and builders. At the same time, many of them are just eyesores on a barren landscape, neglected and crumbling, often dangerous structures that are unwanted and with no possible conversion use. Somebody, long ago, put them up. We just knocked them down. The scrapman really had no part of the heritage argument.

I did have a pang of regret at being part of one particular demolition job. Our company won the contract to level the old Grangetown End enclosure at Ninian Park, Cardiff City's football ground – incidentally, the future home of Cardiff Blue Dragons Rugby League club. A scrapman may be the last person you could accuse of sentimentality, but on this occasion I had mixed emotions as I went into the ground and set to work.

When I was a boy, rugby was a secondary interest for I used to be a real football fan, a regular in that self-same enclosure at Cardiff City FC; and when you go to a place week after week it not only becomes familiar and friendly but seems to take on the human qualities of the spectators, whose two-hour passions, triumphs and disasters are given a weekly airing depending on how the team has played. The Grangetown enclosure was not much of a place, really, and hardly endowed with shrine-like qualities: a crude, even ugly, utilitarian construction of wood, brick and steel with a rusty, leaky corrugated-iron roof. Nevertheless, it meant much to the football faithful of Cardiff. It was part of our lives, a symbol of clubby pride which for all its shabbiness meant in its way as much to us as the splendour of the Civic Centre just up the road does to admirers of much finer architecture.

And here was I, in all my bludgeoning glory, knocking down the whole sacrosanct place, helping to demolish a meeting place not only of an ancient tribal ritual but also of my own boyhood dreams and fantasies.

As we got to work with burning lamp and excavator magnet, those essential tools of the dismantling trade, I couldn't help being aware of the irony of the situation. It was reinforced when, despite the clatter and crashes, the dust and the grime as our gang took the stand apart bit by bit, Cardiff's reserves came out to play a Combination match. Our work contract stipulated that when a game was on, of course, we had to down tools. So, I sat there grimy-faced among the debris and rubble and watched, just like the old days. Everyone should allow themselves the occasional excursion into fantasy; and I have to admit, for a moment or two I was a schoolboy again, mentally shouting and cheering, complaining and chivvying as if I'd paid to go in to watch my favourite football team. Once a fan, always a fan, I reckon (although at this juncture I have to admit that my number-one club was not Cardiff City, but Manchester United, and my hero was Bobby Charlton). 'You'll never take the Grange End!' we used to chant. Another little irony. Nothing had really changed. As in days gone by, when Cardiff were either very, very good or very, very bad, the reserves kept to the script on the day the old Grangetown enclosure came down.

Work stopped, then, when the boys came out to play; but the boss made sure we paid for our little bit of escapism by insisting that we worked an extra two hours in the evening. You might say it was one of my first lessons that there's a price for every pleasure.

Considering the high risk involved in the scrap-recovery business, and in particular my aversion to heights, I was lucky to avoid serious injury. The only work-related accident I suffered was when a piece of scrap went through my wellies early in the week before Wales played Ireland in 1979. For a couple of days I could hardly walk, and I suppose, on reflection, it was foolish to play against the Irish with the injury. I decided not to tell anyone connected with the Welsh team about it. I was afraid that they'd think the risk was not worth taking and that if I was dropped as a consequence there was a real chance I might not regain my place. I didn't want to end up a two-cap wonder. Looking back at the incident, I have to admit it might have been a mistake to cover up the injury and to declare myself fit. I didn't play that well and we had to hang on to win 23–21. It was a bit selfish. I put my own ambition in front of my team-mates, which was wrong. I got away with it – just.

Thinking back to those days on the scrap, I still don't know how I found the courage to crab my way up 100 feet or so to work on huge girders the thickness of a man's body. I shudder to think of the risks I took, and wonder how I managed to close my mind to the height, which I positively hated, and to what could happen if I slipped or made a careless move.

This flirtation with danger as part of the job might explain why I never found rugby rough or truly precarious, although I can see that some people might doubt my sanity when my idea of fun after a day of girder-creeping was to run out in the evening on to a rugby pitch and be prepared for a gang of 16-stone forwards trampling all over me. I wouldn't fancy mountaineering as a pastime or driving a Formula 1 car at 180 mph for a living, but that's a matter of choice, and I'd be the last man to declare that Chris Bonington or Nigel Mansell should be certified.

I was fortunate, then, that during seven years in the scrap business I avoided any real mishap. In fact, the nearest I came to a real purler was not at work, but at home.

By this time, in 1982, I had moved on in the world. I had given up wellies and donkey jacket for grey pinstripe and executive tie, requirements for my new job as a director of General Engineering Services. This company was part of the Erection and Welding Group, owned by local footballer Neil O'Halloran, possibly better known for the fact that he scored a hat-trick on his first appearance for Cardiff City. Neil appreciated how much rugby meant to me at the time, and I shall always be grateful for the opportunity he gave me, not only in terms of job and security, but also to find out about life on the 'other side', where you don't get grime on your hands, you wear a tie and your money goes into the bank every month.

Sue is a down-to-earth, practical person who believes that the basis of a good marriage is the sharing of domestic chores. Usually this means she decides what needs to be done and then tells me to get on with it. One particular day the cleaning of our house windows came top of her hit list. She'd do the ground floor, she said, if I did upstairs. This seemed a perfectly reasonable arrangement, for after all wasn't I well versed in life above ground level whereas the only ladders she knew anything about were those in her tights? Moreover, her confidence in my ability to shin up a ladder and bring a sparkle to our bedroom windows was, to say the least, gratifying. It was with a measure of aplomb that we set about our respective tasks. Me up, she down. It was a lovely day, too, I recall, the sun shining and with little breeze. A good day, I mused, as I went up rung by rung, for Cardiff's match that afternoon against Bristol at the Arms Park. Odd situation perhaps to start thinking about a match. How we would play . . . should we play it off the cuff . . . would Gareth and I test Bristol's defence early on . . . when would we start to stretch them . . . wonder if Gareth would fancy running at 'em . . . might have to talk him into it (as usual) . . . hope it's not too hard a match . . . Welsh squad training next day. My ponderings continued. The sun glinted off the glass. I felt good. Confident. Match tactics OK. Windows nearly done. Sue would be happy. She wouldn't mind now if I stayed on a bit for a few beers after the match. Give and take, marriage, isn't it?

I'm still not sure what happened. One moment the ladder was steady, secure against the roof guttering, the next it began to move. I glanced down. The ground seemed a very long way away. Desperately, I tried to stop the ladder sliding. I lunged at the guttering, hoping to arrest the slide. It didn't. Desperation now gave way to blind panic, and I knew in an instant that nothing could save me except divine intervention. Ladder plus the clinging Holmesy were heading for the ground at a fair rate of knots. A thousand thoughts flashed through my mind as I plunged downwards. Incredibly, what saved me – and maybe saved my life – was a small patio wall, against which the ladder crashed, checking the momentum sufficiently for me to drop off and fall only a few extra feet. I still hit the ground with a resounding thump, but it would have been far worse if the wall had not broken the fall.

The crash – and perhaps my shouts – brought our next-door neighbour rushing to the scene. Now it just happened that Anthony Derbyshire was an out-and-out Cardiff supporter. Quick, too. He summed up the situation immediately. Hardly in the category of ministering angel, though. As I lay in a heap, moaning, he completely ignored me and addressed Sue. 'What on earth do you think you're doing asking him to go up a ladder on a match day?' he asked her in mock seriousness. Sue just gaped. 'I'll be OK,' I gasped, even though at that precise moment I hadn't a clue whether I'd broken a leg or an arm.

'Good,' he replied, giving Sue one of those if-looks-could-kill glares before smartly marching off, leaving me where he'd found me and Sue flabbergasted by his sense of priorities. She soon saw the funny side of it and stood there laughing. I was still prostrate, like a beached whale, wondering if someone, anyone, would chance by and offer help to the intrepid ladder climber in the moment of his greatest humiliation. . . .

Pride, thankfully, was the only real sufferer, and although my legs were bruised and quite badly grazed I reckoned I should still play against Bristol. I'd never live it down in the Cardiff dressing-room if the boys found out why I'd pulled out. Giving a fair imitation of Long John Silver, I struggled through the match, but overnight everything tightened up, so that even with the best intentions there was no chance I could play in the Wales squad session on the Sunday. I turned up and gave some feeble excuse for not taking part. I didn't mention the ladder.

The real injuries in my life, of course, occurred on other fields, and were far more publicised. I shall be discussing them – necessarily at some length – in the next chapter.

7

Injuries

Anyone involved in a physical-contact game, regardless of the level at which it is played, has to come to terms with one thing above all else: there is a likelihood of incurring injury on a fairly regular basis, whether in the form of a slight graze, a bruise, a cut, a torn muscle or tendon, or something more serious like a fracture. These are occupational hazards, and to a rugbyman harsh facts which all players accept.

Since, to my knowledge, no statistics on rugby injuries have ever been compiled, nobody is really aware of how often injuries occur, except in the case of the better-known and more publicised players whose every action is understandably subjected to wide and clinical scrutiny. As a result, certain sportsmen tend to be described, usually by the media, as being injury-prone, that is, more than normally liable to sustain an injury. It is a dismaying diagnosis, suggesting that you are suffering from some totally unknown, incurable, terminal illness and have only a few days left in this world.

Although I could argue that my list of injuries, minor and major, is not abnormal, I have learned not to protest about it. I just accept that some people *think* I'm injury-prone. I am described as such, therefore I am. If this causes resentment or ruffles your sensitivity, no matter. You soon discover that there is nothing you can do or say to change other people's attitudes. The best policy is to shrug, smile and get on with the business of living . . . and playing.

The strange thing is that although throughout my career I seem to have had my share of injuries, some quite serious, I can honestly say that none of them depressed me to the point that I ever considered giving up the game. Setting aside the nuisance element of, say, surgery, treatment and prolonged therapy, injuries really are nothing more than killjoys. They just stop you playing, stop you having fun. Probably they matter more to headline writers than they do to those who suffer them.

Still, I'm in reasonably good (non-rugby) company in this respect. How many times, for instance, has Manchester United's Bryan Robson been written off? I bet he could cover the walls of his loo with the headline cut-outs alone. What of Mark Lawrenson, of Liverpool? His shoulder has come out three times and he's no Quasimodo shuffling around Anfield. What about Seb Coe and Steve Ovett? How many times were their athletic obits written? And when someone like Alan Wells suddenly – 'miraculously' – came back from his particular scrapheap, why were the gasps of surprise confined to the Press box? You could, of course, go on and on, naming hundreds of men and women in a multitude of different sports who have been hit by injury or mishap and thereupon advised to buy white sticks or a wheelchair or increase their BUPA cover. And to think I used to believe it was only politicians who got things wrong over and over again.

Mind you, the medics often don't help. Sports-injury victims go to them for help and reassurance and it rather undermines your belief in the medical profession when they solemnly pronounce: 'You'll never play again.' It's almost as if they're daring you to prove them wrong.

Where injuries are concerned – as in other aspects of life – I'm something of a fatalist. I believe whatever will be, will be. Even so, I am fascinated by the horoscopes in my daily paper: one of my many Piscean weaknesses, so I'm told. And that Russell Grant, he's following me around. We had him, down in Wales, in the *Western Mail* and, lo and behold, that tubby and merry sage has a column up in Yorkshire, too. I can't pretend I understand the jargon about planets in the ascendancy or making influential conjunctions and the like. That's just Greek to me. For me, reading the stars is only a bit of fun. You do wonder now and then when they get things right, when some of the predictions and promises *actually* happen to you. Then you remember the law of averages and realise that all horoscopes are a con really, and you're daft to be reading them in the first place.

Just as daft, I suppose, is having your palm read. I've indulged in that flight of fancy only once. I was enjoying a sort of farewell party with friends in a nightclub in Cardiff just before leaving Wales to go north for my first match for Bradford Northern in November 1985, when a lady, actively encouraged by my pals, approached our table and offered to interpret the lines on my hand. She seemed expert, assured. She took hold of my hand gently, peering down into it like a pawnbroker examining a family heirloom. 'You are going to be very successful,' she declared persuasively. A week later I was in the Bradford Clinic with a dislocated shoulder, after lasting only thirteen minutes in my Rugby League début.

I have been luckier than many players in having sustained comparatively few of those irritating small knocks that keep you out of action for one or two matches. Excluding major injuries, I hardly missed a match throughout the whole of my career, and I was only taken off to be treated for a minor bang on a couple of occasions. Taking that into account, then, and remembering the hundreds of matches in which I've played in seventeen years of rugby, rumours of my proneness to injury will be seen as exaggerated.

The first injury worthy of mention didn't even occur in rugby. I broke an ankle when I was eighteen, playing basketball for Central Youth Club at Bute Road, down near Cardiff docks. In high-risk terms, basketball can't be mentioned in the same breath as rugby. But like many sports in which physical contact is relatively insignificant, basketball, with its inherent speed, its reliance on sharp twists and turns and sometimes a defiance of gravity, is dangerous enough. I played a lot of it as a youth, and was lucky to escape relatively injury-free. Except for that one broken ankle. Some basketball players I know seemed to be in and out of hospital every other week.

The first chapter in the history of my rugby injuries was written in 1976 when I was twenty. It was another broken ankle, and was entirely my fault because I shouldn't have been playing in the first place. Cardiff had picked me as sub for Gareth Edwards in the traditional Boxing Day fixture against Pontypridd at the Arms Park, and the prospect of spending a cold December afternoon sitting out a match on the bench held about the same appeal as going for a swim in the Taff. So, when I was invited to take part that morning in a local fun match for Jimmy Riordan's XV, I couldn't refuse. Cardiff wouldn't have been best pleased had they found out, but what they didn't know about, they wouldn't fret about. . . .

The match lived up to expectations, a pleasant run-about with no pressure and hardly any serious tackling. It was thoroughly enjoyable and I reckoned I'd still be OK and have enough puff left even if I had to play for Cardiff later in the day. Then, two minutes from the end, 'crack', my ankle had gone.

Only then did the enormity of my 'crime' hit me. I'd disobeyed one of the golden rules of my club, and now, with a broken ankle, I'd let them down. I was beside myself with a mixture of guilt and remorse. Obviously I had to convey the bad news to Cardiff as soon as possible so that they could hustle around for a substitute for their substitute. I phoned the club.

'How did you manage to break your ankle on Boxing Day morning?' The question had me squirming with embarrassment.

'Oh, I turned it over running in the park.' The lie came out heavy as lead.

My morning team-mates showered me with sympathy and promises of strict secrecy. No way would they drop me in it with Cardiff, they vowed. Nobly, too, they transported me to casualty at a nearby hospital where they left me, and with 'good luck' and 'see you soon', they all trooped off to a local pub. Any ideas I had of joining them were soon shattered. Because it was holiday time, the hospital was coping with a skeleton staff, which meant I had a tediously long wait before I was even examined. At last someone came and looked me over. There was no chance, I was told, of an X-ray or plaster. Christmas holidays, isn't it? No one was on duty in those departments. Eventually the throbbing ankle was bandaged up, and I was requested politely to return in two days when I'd be given normal casualty attention – which would have been all right but for the fact, I then realised, that the boys had left me alone and there was no one able to give me a lift either to pub or home. Never, never again would I play in a tin-pot morning match, I growled to myself as I hobbled out of the hospital.

It was another four years, in which I must have played in nearly a hundred matches, ten of them in a Wales jersey, before I was to see the inside of a casualty unit again. This time it was in South Africa, 1980. And it wrecked my first tour with the Lions.

The tour had gone marvellously for me. I was fitter than at any time in my life, and with Colin Patterson also in good form, there was keen competition for the scrum-half place in the Tests. I'd scored a try in each of the victories over Eastern Province and Natal, and when I scored another after only two minutes in my third match at Bloemfontein, against Orange Free State, my confidence was sky-high. I was soon jolted back to reality when I got involved in a mêlée and hit the ground with a thump. Out went my left shoulder, but because it popped back almost immediately I decided to play on. It was a rash decision, for the next tackle, by Free State scrum-half Sonnekus, had me writhing in agony. This time I had no option but to go off. I was out of action for over two weeks. It was a thoroughly miserable time, and deadly frustrating because I knew the injury would rule me out of contention for the first Test, which I'd set my heart on. Wearing the Lions jersey in a Test was an honour which I rated on a par with playing for Wales.

On tour, someone's misfortune is, of course, someone else's good fortune. The Test job went to Colin Patterson, the chirpy 5 foot 5 inch Ulsterman who had to give up his job as a solicitor in Newtonards so that he could tour. Colin, a great mate, commiserated with me over my injury. 'Good luck. You'll do a great job,' I told him, and I meant it. Colin, in fact, played pretty well on that warm, bright day at Newlands but the sun didn't shine on the Lions. South Africa scored five tries and we lost 26–22. Davie Serfontein, South Africa's scrum-half, scored the winning try in injury time and as I watched him from the stand, zipping over from a maul, I wondered whether I could have stopped him had I been playing.

That defeat for the Lions, their first in twenty-nine matches in South Africa since 1968, made me even more determined to get back into the fray. The shoulder was still not one hundred per cent, but when the Lions coach, Noel Murphy, asked me how I felt about playing against Eastern Transvaal I replied, 'I'll give it a go.' It must be remembered that at the time the Lions injury list was growing, and my decision to risk all against Eastern Transvaal was influenced as much by that as by personal ambition to try to make the team for the second Test. The wheels came off midway through the first half at the Pam Brink Stadium in Springs. Not the suspect shoulder, but torn ligaments in my right knee. The tour for me was finished. I flew home early in the company of three other casualties, Gareth Davies, Dai Richards and Fran Cotton, though the list was far longer than that by the time the tour ended. The rest of the team gathered outside our hotel to bid farewell to the walking wounded. I don't think I've ever seen so many fixed, false smiles. The jokes were terrible too. Everyone looked as if they were going to a funeral.

During the months that followed, my knee injury cleared up and after cortisone treatment for my shoulder I – ever the optimist – declared myself fine and fit to start the 1980 home campaign. I played for Cardiff against New Zealand and then for Wales against the All Blacks, the best side I've ever played against. They gave us a drubbing none of us will ever forget. My only consolation by now was that my injuries were no longer disabling, and I was at more or less peak fitness again. Then, in December, came the final blow of 1980. Playing for Cardiff against London Welsh at Old Deer Park, I went for a tackle on Clive Rees, the Welsh wing. Now catching someone as quick as 'Whizzer' is a feather in anyone's cap. For a scrum-half like me, with my relative lack of pace, cutting him off was one for the scrapbook. It made the scrapbook all right . . . for the momentum of my tackle propelled both of us with an almighty crash into an advertising hoarding near to touch-in-goal. Whizzer was winded. I was in agony. The shoulder hadn't dislocated, but it was obvious that there was still something drastically amiss with it. 'Holmes to have operation,' the headlines blared ominously. Not a good year, 1980, by any stretch of the imagination.

The operation was carried out by John King, the eminent orthopaedic surgeon. The shoulder joint had calcified and needed clearing out, a straightforward surgical job, I was assured, and so it was. I went into the Albert Dock Hospital in East Ham on a Friday, had the operation the next day and was back home in Cardiff on Sunday. However, the subsequent rest and recuperation inevitably meant that I would miss the whole of 1981 Championship season, which formed the latter part of Wales's Centenary celebrations. It was a year before I played for Wales again, in a full international, against Australia at the Arms Park on 5 December 1981. Before that, thank goodness, there were consolation prizes for wounded warriors: a reappearance in an international jersey against a President's XV in April, and a Welsh Cup match for Cardiff, together with Gareth Davies, when we beat a Bridgend side which included Gerald Williams and Gary Pearce, who had (temporarily, I'm glad to say) taken over the Wales half-back positions.

The injury bug was not to bite again until March 1982. Against England at Twickenham, the malignant spirit which seemed to accompany my every move pointed its wicked finger at my right shoulder, and out it sprang. Gerald Williams took over. Wales lost 7–17, but worse was to follow. A fortnight later, my arm in a sling, I watched in anguish and embarrassment from the stands as Scotland scored 34 points, the highest score ever by any side against Wales in Wales. 'I'll bet you're glad you missed that one,' a spectator remarked to me as I made my way through the mournful multitudes to the Wales dressing-room. I was too upset to reply. I didn't even go in to see the lads to offer condolences. After a beating like that, the last thing players want is half-baked platitudes from someone who wasn't out there sharing the misery; and it seemed wrong to intrude on private grief, particularly when some of the players must have realised by then that they'd made their last appearance for their country. Six were axed, never to play again, and it took another two seasons before my old pal and partner, Gareth Davies, was restored to favour. On reflection, perhaps it was a match to miss.

I wish I had missed the British Lions first Test against New Zealand in Christchurch on 4 June 1983. The jinx struck with a vengeance in this match. Once again, I was prevented from completing a Lions tour, fated to be the only player ever to be sent home twice because of injury.

Curiously, my fate was settled in the second match of the tour, against Auckland. Andy Haden and Gary Whetton had cleaned us out in the line-out (Steve Bainbridge and Steve Boyle just could not cope with the All Blacks number-one choices); and when the same two players were named for the First Test we based our line-out tactics on the assumption that this was an area where New Zealand might establish control, although Bobby Norster and Maurice Colclough were the Lions Test second row. Consequently, the pre-match line-out strategy was to try to avoid Haden and Whetton whenever we could. This meant that on our throw-in, we'd concentrate on two-man line-outs or long throws to the back. Ciaran Fitzgerald's accuracy at the throw-in had caused concern (and comment in the Press) but for the throw to the back the tour captain didn't need a slide-rule. Accuracy wasn't that important. For half an hour, everything worked reasonably well, and there were signs we were building a platform for victory. But for me one cruel piece of ill-luck spelt the end.

Ciaran threw long. Murray Mexted went for the ball, missed, and I leapt up like a line-out jumper to snatch up what should have been a gift of a ball. Unfortunately, I mistimed my jump badly and came to earth like a drunken stork, legs spreadeagled. I felt something go in my knee as I landed. I didn't bother to think about what might be wrong. All I knew was it bloody hurt. If it was painful at the time, it was excruciating later in hospital. After a preliminary examination, which showed ligaments and tendons in a right mess, the surgeons decided they'd wait until next day to probe further.

I was put in a general surgical ward for the night, sharing with about a dozen others, mostly of senior citizen status. Affable and chatty though my ward-mates were to prove during the following days, and good company really, it was a different matter that first night. I was in agony (the medics didn't give me any pain-killers) and I couldn't get a wink of sleep, not only because of the pain but because in their sleep my companions did a fair imitation of a brass-band at practice. The snoring, snorting and oom-pah-pahs from other orifices blared out all around me, echoing off the white-tiled walls. All night it went on, nearly driving me out of my mind. When morning came, and the dreadful nocturnal concert had ceased, I lay in my bed like a wet rag, absolutely exhausted.

'How're you feeling?' one of them enquired considerately from an adjoining bed. I looked at him bleary-eyed. 'Not too bad,' I lied. Had he only known, it wouldn't have taken much for me to have ignored my injured knee, to have leapt out of bed and bonked him and his pals over the head with their bedpans.

We all have to endure some bad moments in our lives. That first night in Ward 3, Christchurch General Hospital, is top of my list by a fair margin.

Still, not all was unpleasant in hospital. Even with a dodgy knee, I was soon chatting heartily with my tormentors of that first nightmare night as if we'd been friends for life. We nattered interminably about rugby, about the tour and most of all about Wales. Flatteringly, they all seemed to want to know about my life back home. I was pleasantly surprised, too, at the number of get-well messages, piles of fruit and other presents that streamed in from the people of New Zealand while I was in hospital. Some came from people I knew, but most were sent by kind-hearted folk I'd never met. I needed cheering up; the good wishes were just what the doctor ordered.

The camaraderie of the ward, and the gifts, also helped to divert my attention from the injury, and its implications. I didn't begin to feel sorry for myself until the surgeon confirmed what I'd already suspected. 'Sorry, lad, but the tour's over for you.'

Back home, a world away, the news reached Susan. She had stayed up into the early hours to listen to the radio commentary of the match, but she hadn't realised how serious the injury was until the next morning. From then on, she telephoned every day, and the nurses cheerfully loaded me into a wheelchair so that I could get out of the ward to take the calls. Obviously it was all a bit of a strain for Susan, particularly after speculation in the newspapers back home that the injury was so serious as to jeopardise my career. One day, inevitably, she broke down and cried when she got through to the hospital. Fortunately, Ikey Stephens, the Bridgend prop, had popped in for a visit and was at hand to take her call. He saw it as his duty to try to cheer her up. 'It's not that bad,' said Ikey. 'You know he did it deliberately, don't you? He was just homesick. He wanted to get back to you, that's all.' By the end of their chat Ikey's charm and quips had perked her up so that she was back to her normal self by the time the phone was passed over to me.

Ikey's intervention was to prove ironic. A fortnight after I left New Zealand, he too was on his way home, with badly torn muscles in his knee.

Within a month of my return the WRU had arranged an operation for me with the Cambridge surgeon, David Dandy, who specialised in sports injuries. 'A typical rugby player's knee,' Mr Dandy concluded after examination. He recommended an anthroscopy, using a relatively new branch of microsurgery which entailed inspecting the damaged area without a major incision. 'There'll be just four little pinpricks,' Mr Dandy promised. There were. I could hardly believe it, for I had been steeling myself for a real carve-up. Even more comforting was his decision not to operate; he'd give the knee a general clean-up, but nothing dramatic or extensive. If I had major surgery, he said, the likelihood was that it would improve my mobility by no more than 10 per cent. The conclusion was obvious.

'Will I play again?' I asked tentatively.

'Yes, I'm sure you will,' he replied. 'But it will be entirely up to you at what level.'

Once Mr Dandy had performed his miracle, I felt a sense of relief. I knew I'd play again, and after all those black moments of depression and doubt only that mattered. Even the prospect of weeks of physiotherapy – normally soul-destroying – was bearable. The mere promise that I'd be back in action was tonic enough. I'd sail through the physio, I promised myself. It helped, too, to know that when I got to the Taly-garn Rehabilitation Centre, just outside Cardiff, I would soon be joined by that other limping Lion, Ikey Stephens, following an operation on his knee. Taly-garn was to have a profound effect on both of us.

Taly-garn has been long established as a post-operative centre for victims of industrial injuries. Naturally, most of the patients came from the Welsh coalfields and the steel industry. The centre had wanted for some time to widen its scope by specialising in the treatment of injured sportsmen, and Messrs Stephens and Holmes were given a hearty welcome. The place was superbly equipped, the staff were considerate and highly efficient, and John Price, the PT instructor attending to Ikey and myself, really put us through our paces. It was no holiday camp.

I was at Taly-garn for six weeks. Compared with the dreadful injuries some of the patients had suffered, my injury was a piffling inconvenience. Their cheerfulness and fortitude were incredible, and humbling. They laughed and joked, but the pain and suffering were written plainly in their eyes and could never be disguised. I've known lots of tough, hard guys in rugby but none, I suspect, would measure up to some of the men at Taly-garn. They had guts and a determination I'll never forget.

Although the starker aspects of Taly-garn helped keep my feet on the ground, my time there was far from dispiriting. It was not all therapy and sweat and labour to get wasted muscle back into harness. Team spirit was the order of each day; and when not queuing up for meals, or helping to collect used dishes and cutlery, we found plenty of other diversions. Ikey and I quickly paired up to become the snooker kings of the centre. We took on all comers and enjoyed some really tense, hard-fought struggles to hang on to the championship. A combination of flair, flukes and inherent competitiveness gave us the edge. There were some moans, though, over the weekly raffle. Ikey and I won the £1 prize so often that the inmates suspected a fiddle – and told us so. Despite that scepticism, I became very friendly with many of the patients, and I still regularly correspond with a few of them, particularly Herbert Staines, an ex-miner from Bettws. Herbert was crippled with arthritis but he had a marvellous temperament, and his earthy philosophy and good common sense made him a wonderful and interesting companion. Our chats were therapy in themselves. If I had one complaint about my daily visits to Taly-garn it was John Price's insistence that, for my last two weeks, I should leave my car in the garage and cycle to and from my home in Llandaff. Nine miles each way isn't much, except when it comes to biking. I'm no King of the Mountains, and I found the morning run to Taly-garn, almost all uphill, tested both my stamina and my patience.

The most curious of all my Rugby Union injuries came in what proved to be my last match for Wales, against Fiji at the Arms Park on 9 November 1985. Wales were much the better side that day and when things are going well a player relishes the opportunity to enjoy himself, to turn on the style, as it were. I was doing just that, playing with plenty of confidence in a sound team performance, when Peceli Gale, one of the Fijian flankers, homed in on me. It was an extraordinary tackle, a real nose-diver, as they say in American Football. His head banged against my right knee and I went down as if someone had shot me. I didn't suspect any serious damage – nor was there – but because Wales were well on top at this point, I deemed it a wise precaution, as captain, to leave the field for treatment. As I limped off, the crowd gave me the most incredible reception, and I wondered if they knew something that I didn't. Within a month I was a Rugby League player, and everyone knew my career with Wales was over.

Inevitably, when a player switches from Rugby Union to Rugby League, and the fee for so doing is a record, the move must attract a lot of attention and publicity. Both I and Bradford Northern were aware of that. It was sound business practice for the club to make the most of the ballyhoo, and to encourage interest in every way; hence the signing on television and the announcement that I'd make my first appearance in a Northern jersey as soon as possible. It was a matter of keeping the publicity pot boiling, which outweighed any consideration of throwing someone with a meagre tactical knowledge of the game in at the deep end, without a couple of preliminary warm-up matches. Even in retrospect, I think it was the right thing to do, not a calculated gamble; raw though I was, I had enough confidence in my rugby experience and ability to believe I could deal with most of the likely circumstances the new game would throw up. Had I believed otherwise I would have told Northern, and I'm sure they'd have respected my caution.

So with the whole world looking on, it seemed, Northern's

newest player went on parade, against Swinton on 8 December 1985. An attendance of 5,257 was nearly treble Swinton's average for the season so far, and their biggest for a league match in nine years. The many Bradford Northern fans were understandably anxious to examine and assess the club's expensive investment; and a lot of friends and supporters, including many of my former colleagues from Cardiff, had journeyed up from Wales. In the circumstances it is hard to imagine a more disastrous début, from everybody's point of view.

Let me stress at once that it was my instinct as a Rugby Union player which brought the world crashing down on my head. It was not due to inherent physical weakness or even an old injury. My shoulder came out of its socket because of a series of events which I'm sure I could have coped with separately, but which in combination made me a helpless victim of illogical fate. It was a freak accident, pure and simple, as anyone who has suffered a similar mishap would confirm.

Naturally, I remember the events leading up to it with some clarity. Swinton chipped through and Dean Carroll and I raced back to cover. Dean picked up, was tackled and I automatically adopted the half-back role. The ball came to me, and here I made my first mistake – I ran – just as I would have done from loose play in Rugby Union. The ball should have gone out to my forwards. Three of Swinton's tacklers, no admirers of audacity, fastened on to me immediately, and one of them grabbed my arm. Mistake number two was trying to yank my arm free, and attempting to stay on my feet as per Rugby Union, instead of going to ground with the tackle and accepting that I'd been held. The player hanging on to my arm followed his instincts – Rugby League, not Rugby Union – and pulled me down. In that simple, ridiculous tug-of-war, out came the shoulder.

Even dafter was that I simply refused to believe it had happened, to give way to that awful, sinking feeling of letting someone, everyone down. So I stayed on, with the shoulder out. I even made a couple of tackles until Phil Ford, my old pal from Cardiff, who was on the wing, shouted to me: 'Come out of the middle, come on, play outside me!' He could see my distress and managed to convey it to Ronnie Barritt, Northern's physio, who

71

raced on to help. By this time, the damage had been done. There was no way he could manipulate it back into place. I didn't think about the pain, or even the embarrassment. For Susan, sitting in the stand, it was even worse.

'What a load of rubbish!' and 'Get him back to Wales!' – the stinging insults rang out from the crowd, and she felt they were aimed directly at her. She told me she felt sick, and sadder than at any time in her life.

Meanwhile I was taking a shower, prior to being taken to the Bradford Clinic. Incredibly, a photographer sneaked his way into the shower room and wanted to take a shot of me naked. I was dumbfounded. I don't think I've felt so angry in my life. I suggested he left quickly, or his camera might quite forcibly be inserted somewhere for which it was anatomically unsuited.

Paul Robinson, one of Northern's directors, drove me to Cottingley, an agonising fifty-minute run from Swinton. 'Don't worry,' he reassured me. 'Everything's going to be all right.' I had to have a general anaesthetic in the Yorkshire Clinic before they could put the shoulder back. Susan then had to drive me home, back to Cardiff, and that was a journey I want to forget, four miserable hours on a wet, bleak winter's night, as cold and friendless as some of the spectators back at Swinton. My shoulder ached and my mind throbbed with the events, the consequences of the blackest day of my life. I was utterly exhausted by the time we arrived home, after midnight. The only grain of comfort in my beleaguered thoughts was that it would never happen again. Improbably, unbelievably, it did.

Five weeks later, on 21 January 1986, in my very next match for Northern – or, more precisely, their A team against Batley A at Odsal – the shoulder came out again. I made a tackle and fell on my elbow, not heavily, but with enough of a jar to jolt the shoulder out from the joint. Like a repeat dream, a bad one, there I was on my way back to the Yorkshire Clinic.

I realised then that I was at the crossroads in more senses than one. Either I submitted to cruel fate and gave up playing, or I should have an operation on the suspect shoulder. Susan and I discussed the situation at length. It had been a bad time for her as well, and I appreciated that I was asking a lot of her if I decided

72

to have the operation. 'You have to do it,' she said eventually. 'You've not only got to prove everybody wrong but you've got to prove it to yourself that you can make it at Bradford.' I knew she was right. I just *had* to show everyone that Terry Holmes was going to make it in Rugby League – and that there was no truth, absolutely none, in all that malicious, cynical gossip about his being injury-prone.

8

Scrum-half

When I was a youngster, I played a lot of my rugby at centre and fly-half, and progressed by natural stages to what everybody considered my strongest and best position – scrum-half. By the time I was sixteen I had specialised in the position, I suppose, and began to mould my game on the best players who were around. It was obvious that I, and those interested in furthering my career, would be influenced greatly by the master of them all – Gareth Edwards. In Gareth's day the vogue was the long pass and because that long pass suited the way the game was then played, any scrum-half aspiring to the top had to develop a similar pass. I was no exception. I wanted to play top rugby so I worked on improving the length of my pass, although in many other areas I was a completely different kind of player from Gareth. My imitation of him was therefore restricted to passing.

As the game developed, however, and the long pass gradually ceased to be so important, being superseded, particularly at international level, by the short, wristy, quick delivery, I found myself at a disadvantage. In fact, when I wanted to speed up my pass, and to work on my 'weak' delivery from right to left, I realised it was too late. I was too set in my ways, although perseverance brought some improvement.

Old habits are difficult to shake and although there are aspects of your game that you can improve – such as kicking – your main armament, your principal source of skill, inevitably remains untouched. I've always been convinced that talents come naturally, that they are intuitive, and that by the time you are playing at senior level the best you can achieve is to hone what skill or flair you have always possessed. Everything else is a compromise and if, for instance, by that stage of your career you

74

have never learned to kick with both feet, you cannot start to learn late in life.

Like a lot of players, I've toyed with the idea of what I'd do if I had my time over again. I've asked myself what I could have done to improve my play, to have made me better equipped to meet the requirements of the modern game. I realise now that, had things been different, I could have adapted, provided I had started early, when I was learning the game. Youngsters today have a much better opportunity of making changes, or learning, and if I were to pass on any advice to a budding scrum-half it would be that, although he should give priority to being right-footed and left-handed, so to speak, *ideally* he should be able to kick with both feet and pass off either hand. Probably without realising it, all scrum-halves find themselves right-foot kickers because, having put the ball into the scrum on the left side their movement towards the back of the scrum and their positioning for the heel naturally encourage a right-foot kick. Yet there are so many other occasions when to be able to kick with either foot is an asset that a one-footed kicker is disadvantaged. The fly-half is always reckoned to be the game's tactician, but a scrum-half, too, must be able to kick well – defensively, clearing up and varying kicks into the box, and using diagonals and garry-owens. Being able to kick with both feet doubles a scrum-half's options.

The complete scrum-half must also be able to pass with equal speed and fluency off both hands. I was a naturally right-handed player, and although my passing was a strong part of my game, I realise how much better I would have been had I been able to pass both sides, like Dave Loveridge. Giving the backs quick ball often makes the difference between scoring and not scoring, and Loveridge was the master in this respect, for he had the option of bulleting them out left or right. Young scrum-halves would do well to copy Dave, who in my view was the best technical scrum-half of my generation. Gareth Edwards, whom I succeeded in the Welsh team, was a better all-round player, a supreme athlete and a gifted footballer, but as the game changed from the 1970s onwards, the quicker passers of the ball gradually came to dominate. In fact, rugby has altered so much that I honestly feel my type of game would have been exposed and would have appeared flawed. I wouldn't have got away with it. I might even have had to play flanker, as so many suggested!

Passing and kicking, however, are only part of a scrum-half's armament. The ability to tackle is often overlooked. It is very important to be able to take men out on the fringes of the set-pieces and in loose play, and a scrum-half who can cover-tackle like, say, Robert Jones, is worth his weight in gold. Robert is an outstanding cover tackler, and you often see him haring back into a position where his intuition and game experience tell him he'll be needed. Often Robert becomes the last man in defence; he has made some telling tackles and has stopped certain tries.

Another ability of the complete scrum-half is in support play. Successful sides in the modern game have support players fore and aft, but a scrum-half often is ideally placed to help sustain movements, linking with his forwards or supporting the backs. Some scrum-halves, having passed, seem to think that their job is over. This is not so, and the more youngsters are instilled with the essentials of support play, the better all-round players they'll become.

I'd certainly like to see the introduction of clinics for today's young players. It would be relatively easy for respective Unions to organise groups of, say, fourteen-to-sixteen-year-old scrum-halves with potential, and to give them the opportunity of ironing out their weaknesses under the tutelage of top players. How young scrum-halves could benefit if taken under the wing of players such as Gareth Edwards and Robert Jones. A lot of senior players would eagerly support such a scheme. If I weren't a pro, I would love to help out.

I suppose the reason I was able to 'disguise' the weakness in terms of the quick pass was that I had the natural strength to concentrate on a different sort of game. I simply did what I was best at: taking on the opposition at the set-pieces, working with my back row in both attack and defence. Commitment is a necessary requirement of that sort of play, and I think I was born with it. There were plenty of knocks, but I didn't mind them, and in fact I thoroughly enjoyed the physical contact. Peak fitness, too, was essential; I don't think I'd have survived had I not been 100 per cent fit for the job.

It was an advantage, of course, that I had an in-bred competitive instinct which was a great asset in learning the art of survival. The scrum-half's operation zone, by necessity, is close to the forwards, and the very proximity of those big, hairy gentlemen means you're at risk every time you have the ball in your hands. You're in danger, too, when you don't have the ball. Most scrum-halves therefore try to get the ball away as quickly as possible, minimising their involvement with the forwards. I eventually became conditioned to physical confrontation. There were times when the Press labelled me a ninth forward. The description was neither accurate nor flattering. I was a scrum-half operating in the only way I could, employing my particular strengths and qualities within the limitations of my game. Occasionally I was criticised, but one thing is sure: I enjoyed myself.

I scored nine tries for Wales, and most, if not all of them, were similar, being scored from short range, either from the side or rear of a scrum, ruck or maul, or because I had closely supported the forwards. These tries came neither by accident nor design. During my whole career for Wales, I played an entirely instinctive role, I did what I thought was the best thing to do at the time. It goes without saying that I was no strategist, even when I was captaining Wales. I didn't kid myself or anybody else that I was directing a great master plan on the pitch. There was much speculation that the Welsh side of my day was tied down by inhibitions and hampered by ultra-cautious coaching. All I can say to that is that no one ever instructed me what to do when I was in the Welsh team. As far as I know, this went for all the others as well. There was a general coaching policy, it's true, but the players were free to play and act as they thought appropriate.

I played under two Wales coaches, John Lloyd and John Bevan. The latter, in my view, came in for a lot of unfair criticism. Under his guidance Wales didn't produce the goods, but that wasn't necessarily John's fault. Some coaches I have worked with were better managers of men than John Bevan, but over all he goes down in my book as the best I've known. He could only work with the material that was available and in my time there was a shortage of talent in some areas which made it difficult for Welsh teams to compete on equal terms with the best around. And to the common rebuke that Wales didn't do very well in the period I'm talking about, I answer that we didn't do too badly either.

Those who criticise, carp and moan, blaming players and coaches, ought to remember sometimes that Wales has won more international matches than any other country. Our time will come again, that's for sure.

The criticism, incidentally, is not entirely outside the game. There are too many grumblers within, players among them, including some friends of mine, who sometimes forget that the game is and always will be bigger than any individual. By the very nature of rugby there will always be small, niggling things that upset the equilibrium. Nothing, let alone Rugby Union, is perfect. I admit that certain things have irked me, but I have always believed that a player, once he has got to the top, should regard that status as a privilege. It is a privilege to belong, to be part of a game which for all its faults and foibles has a unique place in the field of human activity. To my mind, that is a reward in itself. The game owes us nothing. We, the players, owe it everything.

Today's top players have to make immense sacrifices, as I know from experience. But to my mind, if you want to succeed you have to work at it – rugby football is no different from any other aspect of life. I also believe that every player should take a fresh look at his attitude from time to time. He should question his motivation and assess his fitness. After all, the better prepared you are, the more likely you are to enjoy yourself. And enjoyment, job satisfaction if you like, is the name of the game – Rugby Union, Rugby League, or even Ludo.

My own experience proved to me that there were times when, possibly by playing too much, I became jaded. My game was affected. Sometimes I failed to take the necessary steps to revive my flagging interest. In my case, however, the solution generally lay in training. I liked training, which was a great help, but when I felt my reactions were not quite up to par, or needed to work on my strength and stamina, I did something about it. For example, towards the end of my last season in Rugby Union, I sensed I'd lost a bit of sharpness. So each Wednesday and Friday before a match, I'd go out and sprint. It wouldn't be a huge programme as practised by top athletes, but a mixture, say, of ten 50-yarders and ten 25-yarders. It worked while I was at Cardiff and naturally I adopted the same procedure when I went to Brad-ford. Not only were the sprint exercises psychologically import-ant, but I genuinely believe they added a few yards to my pace. The benefits could be measured. Sprinting was not my only concern. I was also working on my stamina, as a matter of course, and I would run six miles or so as and when necessary.

Since Rugby League is in certain aspects a very physical game, I also needed to do some weight training. Fortunately I didn't have to travel to a gym for this; the car was banished to the forecourt and I fitted out my garage to accommodate the equipment. Until I went to Bradford I didn't fully appreciate the value of weight training, which, if nothing else, has made a big difference to my self-confidence. I didn't grow huge muscles like an entrant for a Mr Universe competition, but I was aware of the marked improvement in strength.

All these routines, of course, are additional to the normal training requirements within the club, and are a matter for each individual. What suits me might not suit others. The principle, though, is that if you want to compete at top level you have to make the extra effort. A word of caution, however. You must take care not to overdo the extra training. As with boxers, it is easy to lose the fight in the gym by over-training, by peaking too early or too often.

I have been asked many times to compare the fitness require-ments of Rugby League and Rugby Union. In my experience, they are similar. You don't have to be faster or stronger for either sport. I have always believed that rugby players, of both codes, are among the fittest of all athletes, comparable to professional footballers. On balance I don't think any League player is necessarily fitter than his counterpart in Union. Playing scrum-half, for example, the important thing is to be quick over, say, 10 to 15 yards; that's why I concentrate on training over distances between 25 and 50 yards. I'm not one of those players who runs in tries from beyond the half-way line, so there is no point in doing 100-yard sprints. A wing, on the other hand, would need to work up his pace for the longer runs.

I am also frequently asked to pinpoint the main differences between playing Rugby Union and Rugby League. That's difficult to answer. Basically, as I've indicated, they are completely different games. But I would say the most important distinction – and Rugby Union should learn from this – is the support play. In Rugby League support is fundamental; the game wouldn't work without it, and it means that backs and forwards have to be top-class support players apart from their other individual skills. Probably only the French and the Australian Rugby Union players can match Rugby League support skills – and look where that unique aspect of their play puts them in the world. Union players could learn much in other directions, but there is one valuable lesson that applies particularly to forwards. To be able to run and handle as well as their counterparts in League would be an enormous asset, and would fundamentally change their whole approach to the game.

Finally, on a personal level, my passing, which was regarded as a bit old-fashioned in Rugby Union, actually works very well in League. In League, players generally support and are actually moving on to the pass, and it follows that my flat, long pass is valuable to hit a target that is already building up speed. In Union, the scrum-half's pass was often standing still. The distance I can obtain with my pass also increases options, because by missing out near support players and bringing the wings into operation immediately, I widen the range of the attack, which is difficult to counter, even in a man-for-man defensive game such as League.

9

Gareth

According to Gareth Davies, who tends to be a know-all in these matters, he and I played in partnership together over 200 times in the ten years we were both at Cardiff. If our playing partnership had a permanence about it, so too did the friendship that stemmed from it. Like anyone else, I have many friends, but the close ones you can count on one hand. Gareth – or Majid as we knew him at Cardiff – is one of these.

Even now, as in a sense we have gone our separate ways, we keep in touch, always seeking an opportunity to chat on the phone, or to meet, to take in a few bevvies, to go out to dinner with our wives in a foursome, or to pair up on the golf course. Over 260 miles separate us, but nothing has really changed from our Arms Park days, except that he's retired from playing while I'm still at it, counting the bruises and the blisters. I always told him that I'd last longer than he would. No stamina, like. When occasionally Maj comes up to Yorkshire to see a bit of Rugby League, I get the impression that he has a wee twinge of regret that he threw his boots into the cupboard before he reached thirty.

Not that he has cut his ties completely with Rugby Union. Nowadays he wears a Barbarians' alickadoo tie, although, from what he tells me, being a committeeman mostly means spending a lot of time on the telephone trying to rustle up players when someone pulls out of a Baabaas match at the last minute because of injury. What with the occasional newspaper column, commentaries on rugby – in Welsh, mark you – and frequent appearances on TV chat and quiz shows, he's a very busy fellow. When does he find the time to go out and have a round of golf, I wonder?

Truth to tell, Gareth would far rather have been a golfer than a rugby player. Like me, he took up golf late in life, and he's fallen in love with it. Albert Francis, the Cardiff groundsman, used to give both of us a lot of coaching, and I can vouch for his expertise. Most of my improvement on the golf course I can put down to Albert's tips. However, he tells me he's now given up on Gareth.

'Gareth doesn't need any more help,' says Albert. 'He now knows more about the game than I do. Well, at least he *tells* me he does.'

That about sums Gareth up. Super-confident. Even if he's not had a good round, he'll persuade you he has. That's exactly how he was when we played rugby together. Looking back, I reckon I learned an awful lot from Gareth about being positive and assertive on the rugby field. So did many of our colleagues at Cardiff. Even when we were being well beaten, Gareth never believed we could lose. His optimism only died when the referee blew the final whistle. He won more than his share of games for us because he wouldn't admit defeat.

His confidence and optimism, however, were not the only qualities that stamped him as one of the best-equipped players of my generation. He was absolutely dedicated to rugby. All the time that we were at Cardiff, I don't think he ever missed training except for a legitimate reason, and he gave more to the club than any other player that I knew. My commitment to Cardiff was understandable. I was a local boy. It was expected of me. Gareth was an outsider, from West Wales. Yet his enduring loyalty and devotion to the club were recognised by the Arms Park faithful who regarded him as one of their own. He was a favourite both with the 'in' crowd in the south stand and the hardy and critical regulars of the terraces. They could make life very difficult for some players, if they suspected they were not giving of their best. It never happened to Gareth.

Not that Gareth was a do-or-die character; on the contrary, self-preservation often was uppermost in his mind. As someone reared on the necessity and desirability of tackling, and tackling hard, I feel I am qualified to judge on this aspect of the game. Tackling obviously was never a compulsory subject on the curriculum down at Gwendraeth Grammar. If there was a flaw in

Gareth Davies, rugby player, it was that. Did he defend himself in this respect? Not a bit. He admitted it. 'I just don't *like* tackling,' was his stock phrase to everyone, coach, selector and committeeman alike.

Barry John (another Gwendraeth product, incidentally) used to describe himself as a fingertip tackler. Gareth didn't even bother with such subtleties. He would only make a tackle, so he'd tell you, if he had to. Or if he couldn't get out of the way. I don't remember any player who kept his hands in his shorts pockets as often as he did. In such circumstances he was a cross between a traffic policeman waving opponents through or a naturalist with a butterfly net, tiptoeing towards his quarry. 'Why didn't you bloody tackle him?' I would demand. 'Too cold, boy. My hands were freezing.' Gareth always had an answer. Eventually I gave up asking him. Like the Cardiff crowd, I got used to it. In any event, he didn't lose many games for Cardiff, and undoubtedly won a lot for us, which in the final analysis is how we all judged him. He was a brilliant match-winner, one of the best I've known. If we needed a dropped goal or a penalty in the last minute, you could rely on Majid. A regular Paul Daniels, pulling something out of the hat when it mattered. And it was not just kicks either. If we needed a try, he could conjure one up with a slick pass, a reverse pass or an inch-perfect kick for the wing. He'd then kick the conversion from the touch-line!

Gareth was a fly-half of many talents. He didn't possess the dazzling footwork of, say, Phil Bennett, or the Houdini-like deception of Barry John. Benny, hunched shoulders, chin jutting out, head bobbing and weaving like a featherweight boxer, tended to lean forward, following his head. He'd carve out a gap and in a flash he was through it. B.J. on the other hand had an upright stance, seemingly sliding through openings sideways. Gareth was, if anything, even more upright than B.J., and like him was deceptively quick off the mark – which is very important for a fly-half. His elegant running, apparently so effortless, suggested he was merely cruising, and probably this impression was one of the reasons for the unfair criticism he endured, particularly when in a Wales jersey. How often was he applauded for being a shrewd tactician, or for his ability in getting his three-quarter line moving? Don't go by my word. Ask any centre who played outside him for proof of his quality in timing and giving of a pass. There weren't many better in my time.

Considering the responsibility of his position, and the pressure that is always on a fly-half, Gareth's calm was monumental. As far as I'm concerned, one of his unique attributes was his extraordinary ability to take a pass, any sort of pass: inches off the ground, high over his head, yards behind him, or in front, it didn't matter. I gave him plenty of practice. Perhaps that's why he was so good, and why the media talked of our telepathic understanding.

In many ways Maj was a throwback to a period when the game was played entirely for fun. He had an incredible ability to shrug off a mistake or a palpably wrong move. If he made a blunder, he never let it worry him. He was always laughing and joking on the field, and the occasional snide remark to a colleague or an 'in-house' quip would have us in stitches. The opposition must have wondered sometimes whether they were playing against a gang of refugees from a lunatic asylum.

Gareth had joined the club from Llanelli – or, to be precise, from UWIST, where he was a student. I'd been a member of the club for two years by then, a novice flexing uneducated muscles in the Youth side. Cardiff's first XV seemed a long way off at the time, hardly a prospect even to be considered, what with Gareth Edwards ruling supreme, and with Brynmor Williams waiting in the wings to take over from him.

I don't think Gareth had any notion of joining Cardiff at all. Like most West Walians, he'd set his sights no further than Llanelli and Stradey Park where he'd played several times before coming to Cardiff to study. Llanelli certainly wanted him to continue his association, but he was finding it very hard to travel back and forth, particularly for midweek training. It was Barry John who suggested that Gareth, at the time struggling in the fly-half position, might find a place at Cardiff. The prospect of playing outside Edwards, one of the all-time greats of the game, was the clincher, and he joined. Llanelli were less than pleased to lose one of their own. One committeeman told him disdainfully: 'You'll learn more sitting in the stand than you will playing at Cardiff!'

It was, of course, a heaven-born opportunity for an eighteen-year-old to play outside someone of the calibre of Gareth Edwards. And when the great man wasn't there, he was able to team up with another future international, Brynmor Williams. Both Brynmor and Maj spoke Welsh fluently, which in a club such as Cardiff was something of a rarity. By the time I came along to challenge for a first XV place, Gareth, thanks to such scrum-half tutelage, was the finished product. I must say it made my life easier that Gareth knew his job in those first few seasons.

It took a while for Gareth and myself to become friends as well as colleagues on the field. He was a student and I was working for a living, knew many local lads and had other interests outside the game. We both had one thing in common, however, and discovering this somehow helped forge the bond of friendship and mutual understanding. Like me, Gareth had been born of working-class parents, and we had both grown up in an environment of some hardship. His father was a coal-miner, an anthracite man, mine was a docker-cum-sailor. And in his family, too, the impetus to follow a sporting career came from his mother. I became very fond of Gareth's mother, a delightful little lady, who, whenever Gareth and I played together for Wales, would invariably provide a bag of Welsh cakes for us to share before we went out to do duty for our country. I greatly enjoyed accompanying Gareth on a visit to his parents' spick-and-span home in Tumble. It was always tea, and Welsh cakes, and long yarns and homespun philosophy from Elvet, Gareth's father. We'd talk a bit about rugby, and boxing, and the pits – politics, too, both local and national. They were lovely visits, and I'll never forget them.

When I think back over my association with Gareth, I realise we grew up together, moving from boyhood to manhood in defined stages. Our first match together for Cardiff in 1975 – his first for the club, my second – was really a baptism for each of us. We were thrown in at the deep end, in every sense, at Pontypool Park, a ground on which all your credentials for playing this game of ours are minutely examined. If I didn't know it before, I certainly knew it during the game. Gareth was a natural, a match-winner. If he had any nerves, or worries, he didn't show it, and he proceeded to beat Pontypool almost on his own. A couple of dropped goals and a couple of penalty goals quelled their competitiveness and gave Cardiff a result that they could never rely upon on that same ground for the next ten years. You have to be good to beat Pontypool on their own patch.

My own recollections of the match are best summed up in Max Boyce's words – 'Duw, it's hard, harder than you'll ever know'. While Gareth was doing the business, as it were, in the middle of the park, I was much closer to the Pontypool forwards – and to the action. You get to know opposition forwards extremely well at close quarters, which is part of the job, of course, as a scrum-half. It took me some time, in fact, to adjust to the pace of the game; everything I did came out of the Youth team guidebook, the only rugby that I'd so far experienced. I soon discovered what a gap there is between Youth and first-class rugby. It was a clinical and salutary first lesson. After feeling my way tentatively for twenty minutes, I decided it was time to offer some variation from snap kicks to touch and feeding Gareth. From a line-out, I said to myself, 'Well, let's have a go at their back row,' and I launched myself on an angled run towards their loose-forwards, just as I had done so often for the Youth. It was a purely instinctive act. The next thing I knew was 'whap' – I had been hit by Terry Cobner and down I came like a bag of wet cement. That wasn't all. In a flash, Cobs had turned me over, prised the ball from my grip and was away, driving into Cardiff territory. I could hardly believe my eyes. Terry Holmes certainly grew up that day.

The experience hardened my attitude to playing against Pontypool, for over the years taking on their back row became something of a challenge. Nothing changed in that respect. After Cobs came a whole host of tough, hard flankers and I used to have some tremendous set-tos with them. I had particular regard for Chris Huish, who was not very tall but built like Popeye with broad shoulders and big muscular arms. Chris, with his bruiser's flattened nose, was a great character, one of the strongest players I ever encountered. I like to think I got the better of him,

86

but it wasn't very often. Chris hailed from Blaenavon, a mining village nestling in a bleak and desolate fold in the hills above Pontypool, but what a breeding-ground for players. Blaenavon not only produced Huish, but Cobner and my old pal and Wales colleague, John Perkins – forwards all of them, granite-hard and impervious to pain and punishment – not to mention the village's greatest son, Ken Jones, once Wales's record-breaking sprinter and wing.

During the next couple of seasons Gareth and I played together only intermittently and it was not until Brynmor had left to join Newport and Gareth Edwards finally called it a day that we became accepted as the Cardiff half-backs. So we were still comparative strangers when we toured Australia with Wales in 1978, winning our first caps. I was something of a shock selection for that tour – neither Gareth Edwards nor Phil Bennett was available – and the Press gave me number-two billing behind Brynmor. The day the tour party was announced, Cardiff were playing the Barbarians at the Arms Park, and I was on the bench. Edwards, however, pulled out at the last moment and I took the field to team up with Maj. On tour, Brynmor played with Gareth in the First Test at Brisbane, but I got the nod for the Second Test at Sydney. As far as the rest of the world was concerned, the Holmes–Davies partnership was on the map – although considering the results in Australia we did not exactly set the world on fire. However, our time was to come. The Australian disappointments were well and truly put behind us when within nine months we were celebrating a Wales Triple Crown and Championship.

It was inevitable that as our relationship developed on the field – training and playing together for Cardiff and Wales – a friendship should also emerge off it. We were in each other's pocket in more senses than one, and hardly a day went by when we didn't meet up for one thing or another. The final tie to our off-the-field association was knotted by our wives. Helen and Susan had become regular watchers at the Arms Park, and when they became friends, social activities were regularly pencilled into our family diaries. We discovered we had many mutual interests. The lads favoured sampling different restaurants and wine bars while the ladies were happy to play alternate hostesses at home. It was a good life, for all of us, and I know that Susan and I cherished those times above all others.

Obviously, the closer Gareth and I became, the more we confided in each other. Whenever a problem occurred, no matter how serious or personal, each took it for granted that the other would be there to offer opinion and advice. In time we got to know each other so well, with trust as the cornerstone, that we were almost like brothers.

Occasionally we had to make joint decisions. By the time, for instance, we were established in the Welsh team, our reputation as a partnership had spread much further afield. We received several offers to play elsewhere – as a pair. The most significant of these offers was from South Africa, and a very attractive package it was. We both felt flattered that we were rated so highly and we gave the offer very serious consideration. As young married men, just starting out in business, and now offered jobs, houses and apparent security for life so long as we played rugby, we were vulnerable in the best sense. We discussed the situation thoroughly, consulted our wives and eventually said a reluctant 'no thanks' to South Africa. Gareth's chief objection, and a perfectly valid one, was doubt as to what would happen if one of us were seriously injured. My scruple was much more mundane. At the time, my ties with Cardiff – city and club – were so strong that I felt unable to contemplate a move away, no matter how attractive the offer. Probably, too, neither of us was prepared to go without the other. So, by mutual agreement, we stayed. When, ultimately, I did move away, to Bradford, Gareth had already told me that he intended giving up playing within a year.

Nevertheless, when I received the offer from Bradford, I went to Gareth, outlining the details that were privy at the time only to my wife Susan and the Bradford directors. 'What do you think?' I asked him. 'Should I go?' Gareth had of course been aware that I had received several offers to play Rugby League over the years. At best he had advised caution, at worst delaying tactics. This time, he had no reservations: 'You must go, Ombre. The offer is far too good to refuse.' When at length he

y passing has been the subject of much discussion, and criticism, during my career,
d if I had to defend myself it would be to admit that I am not long, quick or fluent
f both hands. Like a lot of players of my generation – and as illustrated – I am
re controlled and stronger at passing from right to left, than from left to right,
cause I am naturally right-handed.

Spot the fly-half. That's him, or rather me, sitting bottom right in the team photograph of the Cardiff Schools Under-11s side of 1968 at Cardiff Arms Park.

Altar boy (second left, second row) at St David's Cathedral, Charles Street, 1967.

Above left *The Bishop Hannon School Under-15s Sevens squad of 1970–1. Although I was still an Under-14 player and somewhat smaller than my colleagues, I managed to hold my place.*

Above right *With Gareth Davies during a practice session at Murrayfield's training ground, the day before we played for the Barbarians against Scotland, 26 March 1983.*

Below left *Father Dai tries to get a reluctant three-year-old to give a smile for the camera.*

Below right *Bedraggled or not, a night to remember, 21 March 1975. As captain of Cardiff & District Youth, I am presented with the D. G. Griffiths Trophy after we had beaten Bridgend 16–0. The next day I made by debut for Cardiff against Newport.*

Captain of Welsh Youth v. France at Pontypool Park, 12 April 1975 – a match none of us who played will ever forget, for we hammered the French 31–11. I scored two tries.

A moment of respite during Cardiff's match against the Barbarians, Easter 1979.

A moment to cherish for any Welshman – leading Wales out as captain at Cardiff Arms Park.

No, not a victory salute, but a captain telling his players to get back quickly and keep up the pressure after we'd scored a try, Wales v. England, 20 April 1985.

A moment when I felt I was playing England on my own, at Cardiff Arms Park, 3 February 1983. Peter Winterbottom has put in the initial tackle, which makes me airborne, but Nick Jeavons, Steve Boyle and Steve Bainbridge reckon on lending a hand.

The Welsh forwards, with Alan Phillips and Rhodri Lewis prominent, tie up the French back, Cardiff Arms Park, 6 February 1982.

Handing off Bill Beaumont during Wales's Triple Crown victory over England at Cardiff, 17 March 1979 – a cherished memory.

Wales's flying wedge has its reward at Lansdowne Road, 23 January 1982 – yours truly goes over for a try against Ireland. Fergus Slattery, mouth agape, doesn't seem to believe it, and for some reason Ciaran Fitzgerald is more involved in getting some scrummaging practice in against the referee.

A *try for Wales against the Maoris, despite the close attentions of Mike Clamp and the atrocious weather.*

above left *Managing to get the ball away in the nick of time as Tony Neary and Mike Rafter try to sandwich me, England v. Wales at Twickenham, 16 February 1980.*
above right *Cardiff v. New Zealand, 1978, and my first confrontation with the great All Black scrum-half, Dave Loveridge.*

Enjoying a joke and a laugh with children outside James Street Police Station, Cardiff Docks.

Susan puts on a brave smile at our wedding on Easter Monday, 20 April 1981, at St Mary's Church, Canton. My damaged eye, which caused much amusement to everyone at the wedding but Susan, had been received against the Barbarians two days earlier. We'd postponed the wedding so that I could play.

Brothers-in-law Tommy and Philip Foley give some help in holding up a girder during a work shift with TJ Contractors.

Proudly displaying the Rugby World 1983 'Player of the Year' Trophy. Unfortunately, that was the last time I saw it. Sometime between the presentation in London and my return to Wales it disappeared!

Gareth Davies appea
sceptical of my
ability to hand off
a Swansea flanker.

The Cardiff changing rooms after our 1984 Schweppes Welsh Cup Final victory over Neath.
Jeff Whitefoot, Scotty, Majid, Bobby Norster (with cup), Alun Donovan and Owen Golding
look pretty pleased with life. I'm wearing Jonathan Davies's jersey.

Being helped off the pitch at Bloemfontein after damaging my shoulder playing for the Lions against Orange Free State, 24 May 1980.

...ne of the low points of ...y career. Stretched out ...ith a knee injury in a ...hristchurch Hospital in ...ne 1983, an injury which ...ded my touring with ...e British Lions.

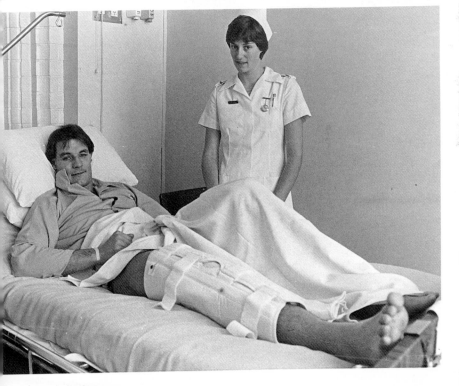

In Bradford Northern colours, I am facing a challenge from Tony Cotterall and Neil McCulloch of Leigh. Wayne Race, the Bradford Northern wing, is in support.

Mick Burke and Paul O'Neill put a check on my progress, Bradford Northern v. Widnes on 16 November 1986. I am wearing red because of the clash with the Widnes colours.

Paul Hume, the Widnes scrum-half, is fractionally too late to stop me getting the ball away for Bradford Northern, 16 November 1986.

Bradford Northern v. Hunslet at Elland Road in the Yorkshire Cup, 14 September 1986. Roy Milton and I wait for the ball to come out of the scrum.

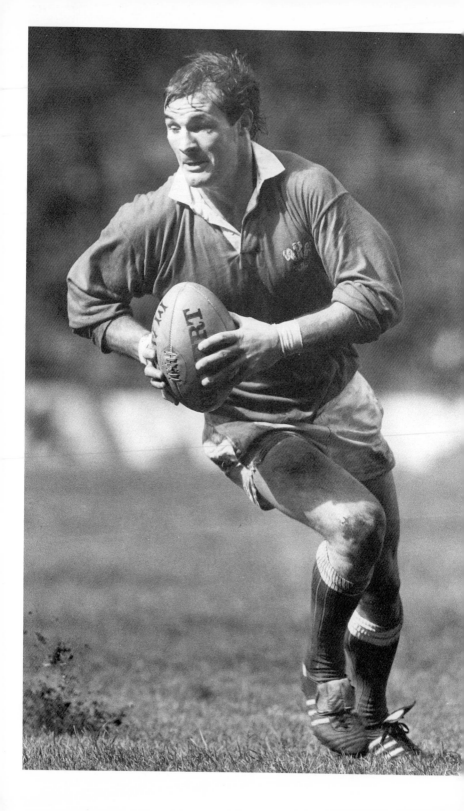

realised I was going to accept, like the good building-society manager that he is, he was quick to point out the advantages of investing with National & Provincial. I could hardly refuse. He always had a persuasive way with him – I bunged a bit across his counter just to keep his figures good.

As I've said, Gareth was one of the great unflappables. Nothing seemed to worry him. In fact, I can recall only one occasion when his calm detachment deserted him. That followed the notorious decision by the WRU selectors to name A. N. Other for the fly-half place in the Welsh side against England in 1985.

Gareth, it will be remembered, was the man in possession. He'd been recalled to the Welsh team after three years in the wilderness and had played in the opening internationals against Scotland, Ireland and France. I was captain of Wales at the time, so I was somewhat embarrassed when the selectors named me and thirteen others, declaring that they wanted to look over all the candidates for the fly-half position at the weekend. My heart sank when I heard the announcement. I felt for Gareth, because although he had some doubts whether he'd keep his place (we had lost to Ireland and France), he was quite unprepared for the quirkish A. N. Other selection. He rang me. He was bitterly upset, pointing out that he would much have preferred to be dropped than to be left not knowing whether he was wanted or not. It was as if they were making him a scapegoat.

'I don't think I can take it,' he confided. 'I think the best thing for me to do is quit international rugby altogether.' Did I think that was the right thing to do? Was it wise? I had to tell him that it was really not a decision that I could take for him. As Wales's captain, and as Gareth's confidant, obviously my loyalties were divided. On the one hand, I had been invested with a responsibility by the WRU, which implied 100 per cent support for them in all things; on the other, a dear and close friend seemed to have been a victim of a gross piece of mis-management. I did my best to balance my awkward situation. Eventually, but reluctantly, I told him that in my considered view he was doing the right thing to quit before A. N. Other's place was filled. I added that I would have done just that in the same circumstances. It was not my responsibility then, or now, to point an accusatory finger over an unsavoury episode. In retrospect, I think it could and should have been handled with a show of diplomacy by the powers-that-be. Why they announced the side at all baffled me; they could, and should, have held it over until they had seen all the fly-half candidates, Gareth included. Gareth had always given of his best for Wales and, let's face it, he had captained them. For those reasons, I think he deserved at least an explanation or a phone call to warn him of their actions. Unfortunately no one had bothered to contact him. It was a decision which left him utterly devastated, and for a long time he was bitter about it. One consequence of a widely publicised incident, however, was that it made many people in the WRU recognise their failings in communication. I'm told on good authority that nowadays there is a much better rapport between officials and players.

Interestingly, a few days after Gareth had made his 'I quit' announcement, he played for Cardiff against Swansea at the Arms Park. He was given a fantastic reception by the crowd as he ran out on to the field. I've never heard the Cardiff crowd so warmly vociferous for one player. Trust Maj, too. He played brilliantly that day, outclassing, incidentally, one of the other candidates for the Wales job – Malcolm Dacey. Yet the selectors had the last word. They replaced A. N. Other not with Malcolm, but with a youngster, then relatively unknown, one Jonathan Davies, from Neath. The king is dead; long live the king. That's rugby.

When I look back over Gareth's playing career, I'm reminded how well he played for Wales. He'd be the first to admit he made a few mistakes, tactically, when wearing the Welsh jersey, but there can't have been many fly-halves with a greater pride in representing their country. To play for Wales was one of the greatest events in his life, the pinnacle of a long and illustrious playing career, and he never once failed to do his best. It meant too much to him. He was loyal, determined and committed, and if things didn't always go right when he wore Wales's No. 10, it was never because of a lack of effort on his part. In my opinion, his greatest game for Wales was against England at Twickenham in 1980 – the Paul Ringer match.

The Welsh forwards that day were magnificent, but they'd be

the first to admit that they were only able to keep the pressure on England because of Gareth. He was brilliant, and his tactical kicking out of hand was flawless. Wales, down to fourteen players when Ringer was sent off, had no right to dictate territorially, but they did because of Gareth, who kept rolling them back with monster kicks. I don't think he failed to find touch once. We lost, but very nearly won. Had we done so, Gareth might properly have been given the credit for it. Me? I don't think I've worked so hard in any match. I was shattered at the end.

Gareth scored 40 points for Wales in twenty-one appearances. His chief regret, he admitted to me, was that he failed to score a try. I used to try to console him. 'I'd have loved to have dropped a goal for Wales,' I'd say to him. A more serious self-reproach concerned the match against Scotland at the Arms Park. Wales lost by 34–18, and Gareth was one of several whose heads fell. I've never been convinced where the fault lay for his, one of the most humiliating defeats in Welsh rugby history. It's possible that Gareth, in his role as play-maker, and John Lloyd, the coach, succumbed to popular pressure to play an open and expansive game. Against Scotland, one of the best counter-attacking sides of my experience, it was a disastrous strategy. Wales made a series of mistakes and the Scots capitalised on them. I have always believed that the only time you should even consider throwing the ball about willy-nilly in an international is when you have the other side beaten, with plenty of points on the board. It makes no sense whatsoever to go out on the field with that express intention. Internationals are about winning. It's nice to win well, but what everyone remembers in the end is the result. Nothing else matters.

Gareth must have been aware of the danger of a loose approach, and he has since admitted he should not have allowed himself to be swayed away from sensible rugby, and his own normal style of play. He was equipped to change the tactics, but by the time he realised what had to be done, Scotland were out of sight. Thank goodness, nobody could blame me. I didn't play in the match. I was injured.

I suppose my chief disappointment in the long time Gareth and I were in harness was that although we played together in some very good sides – Cardiff, Wales and Barbarians – we only once wore British Lions jerseys together; and that was for a mere twenty minutes, too, against Eastern Transvaal in 1980, because Gareth then went off with an injury. We had played together for Cardiff in South Africa, and that was a great experience. In 1980 both of us were probably in our prime, and we couldn't have been fitter or better prepared. To have had the opportunity of playing a Test together for the Lions would have satisfied the lust we had for the game.

This disappointment can be extended, in fact, to include John Scott. In my ideal world, Scottie, Gareth and I would have toured together with the Lions and appeared in Test matches as a unit. Yet Scottie, one of the great No. 8s of my generation, was never considered good enough to wear a Lions jersey. That was an incomprehensible omission by the Lions selectors. Gareth has a pretty controversial explanation for the reason why Scottie was bypassed, but I can't stand witness to that declaration. What I do know is that Scottie was the third corner of a triangle which greatly influenced the way Cardiff played over the years. We were in many ways the linchpin of all Cardiff's constructive play, dovetailing and complementing one another in a manner which would surely have been an asset to a touring side, and could have had a profound effect on the way that team played.

It has been said that Gareth and I enjoyed a telepathic understanding, and I suppose that's right. Towards the end of our partnership I didn't even have to look where he stationed himself to receive a pass; he was always perfectly positioned. In another way, I also had a telepathic relationship with Scottie, and we had many more variations on a theme than might have appeared. It is enough to say that I scored a lot of tries for Cardiff because of Scottie, who frequently could have scored many of them himself. We worked hand-in-glove at the back of scrum, maul and line-out, and we developed an innate sense of the other's intentions and positioning. He would have been a tremendous asset to the Lions because, in fact, he played his best rugby on tour. He was consistently good for Cardiff on the club circuit, but abroad he was that much sharper, fitter and more forceful.

10

Cardiff One

When I reflect upon it, the most incredible feature of my life in rugby football was that the son of an ordinary working-class man should have emerged from the relative obscurity of a Cardiff back-street to captain one of the world's great clubs, and then, equally unbelievably, should have followed by becoming captain of his country. Somebody up there, in Cardiff and WRU committee room, must have liked me.

It seems only yesterday that I first arrived at the Cardiff club, a shy, nervously hesitant teenager, a bit short on chat and even less on worldly knowledge, and wondering in all my puny innocence whether I'd ever be good enough as a player and whether there would ever be a place for me in this great club. Many players aspire to play for Cardiff: only the good, or the lucky ones do. The Arms Park, after all, was hallowed ground, a place of heroes whose names and achievements were written large in the history of the game.

Nor, at the time, were they just names I'd vaguely recollected from schoolyard day-dreams. Inside the clubhouse itself, these heroes of another age were everywhere, their portraits, caps, jerseys and other memorabilia adorning oak-panelled walls in a wonderful mosaic that for a youngster like myself held an almost forbidding quality. Players like Darch and Tanner, Willis and Lloyd Williams, and Edwards, the great Gareth, seemed to look down at me and demand: 'And what are *you* doing here?'

I joined Cardiff Youth when I was sixteen, with not very much of a past and only the next day to look forward to. It was a strangely disquieting time of my life, not only because of the usual teenage stresses and insecurities, and uncertain job and career prospects, but because I really had no idea in which direction I ought to be heading. I had a lot of energy, a certain amount of street-wise native cunning and inherent toughness, but they all needed channelling. Only now, much later and, I hope, a little wiser, do I fully realise and appreciate what it meant to me to join Cardiff and how much it influenced me. There I was given guidance and a sense of purpose; and in a sense the many gaps in my education were filled by mingling with and listening to the people who made the club such a vibrant, compelling place – players, officials, ground staff and supporters.

Loyalty to these people – and thus to the club – and the meaning of friendship were of course by-products. The only way I could give anything back to Cardiff, to reciprocate, was to do my best on the field as often as possible, and that attitude became second nature to me. Let's face it, except for, say, baseball and basketball, the only thing I was any good at in those teenage days was playing rugby. The blue and black jersey was to add another dimension to whatever instinctive skill I might have acquired. I went to Cardiff as a pimply-faced, guileless youth with long, straggly hair and came out a man with the confidence to take on the world – even though the hairline has receded a bit in the process. My personality – defective though it might still be – and my character were moulded there. With the notable exception of the accent, a lot of my rougher edges were knocked off at the Arms Park finishing school, and I discovered, for instance, that the most interesting things in the world were, firstly, people, and then ideas. All that in a rugby club; it seems amazing, but it's true.

But it is more than that, much more. Without Cardiff, and rugby, it is quite possible that I might have ended up at best an Arthur Daley with a Kar-diff accent, and at worst a mindless yob or a no-gooder. I honestly believe your fate can be determined by the side of the street you walk on and the people you happen to meet. Cardiff prison is just down the road from the Arms Park and it's full of blokes who took the wrong road and made the wrong associations.

I owe my present security and status entirely to that club and to this great game; and if in this book I occasionally lapse into sentimentality, I hope I shall be forgiven, and understood. I have a debt to rugby that I can never repay in words. Rugby has been my life and I can't imagine how things would have panned out without it.

Now that I'm earning my living from rugby, it is interesting to reflect that for most of my life in the game, that is, in Rugby Union, I didn't get a brass farthing for playing. Strange to say, I'm glad it was like that. My Rugby Union was pure pleasure; I never wanted to be paid for it. I'm pretty sure that whatever financial adjustments Rugby Union makes in future, a club like Cardiff, a bastion of amateurism, will be one of the last to agree to pay players anything other than expenses. And I'm willing to bet, too, that their Scrooge-like attitude to this matter won't change very much whatever happens in other clubs or at international level. Nobody ever grew rich, in a financial sense, playing for Cardiff, and nobody will in the future.

By other clubs' standards, Cardiff's attitude to expenses is extraordinary. If they weren't legitimate, you didn't get them. If, like me, a player lived in the city proper, he could reckon on £1.50 a week expenses, never more, never less. The sum was based on the price of a bus fare to and from the ground for training and for matches. You could come by Rolls-Royce if you wished, or riding an elephant. You'd still only get the bus fare. Over the years, stories have been told about how much players get from clubs in Wales: cash in boots, in brown envelopes or secreted away in jock-straps. It may well have happened. I know for certain, however, that it *never* happened at Cardiff. The Scottish Rugby Union are supposed to be the last stronghold of amateurism; they're amateurs all right in comparison to Cardiff where a penny is a penny and won't be spent on anything other than the club itself. I understand that Cardiff City Council have recently upped the price for use of a public toilet to 10p. All I can say is that Cardiff players caught short *en route* to the ground had better keep their legs crossed, because they'll never get the money back from the club.

Mind you, Cardiff *do* look after the players, but in well-defined ways, within the strict by-laws of the WRU. There were 'perks' in the form of cost-free overseas tours, every two years, and occasional bonuses such as a new pair of boots or a tracksuit. We also had some free beer. Not a lot. But some.

Let me say, however, that I wholly accepted Cardiff's approach to expenses. No matter how good a player you thought you were, or how good others rated you, the rule on expenses was strictly and fairly applied across the board. Every player in the club, star or not, was treated in precisely the same way. If someone tried to buck the system, he'd soon be shown the door. In fact, only in the last couple of years with Cardiff did I even bother to claim expenses at all. In the early days – before they gave everybody a rise! – the figure was a flat £1 a week; even for someone like me, careful with the pennies you might say, it seemed such a piffling amount that it wasn't worth the trouble. Most of the first XV players felt the same. You joined Cardiff and you accepted their rules.

Rugby Union also taught me another important lesson of life: if you accept the pats on the back, you've got to take the kicks in the groin as well. I can understand, however, that some players might have cause to think differently. For instance, a player's future at the club would sometimes be determined by his relationship with the Cardiff crowd. Your average Arms Park fan is generous in his appreciation and praise for good play and good players, and that applies to home or visiting sides. Paradoxically, though, he can also turn nasty, pouring on the verbal vitriol, and making life thoroughly miserable for some poor soul. No one knows why from time to time a player is singled out for such treatment: it just happens. There have been times when I've known I haven't played well, or have made a real bosh of something, and dreaded the crowd's reaction: 'My word, they're going to give me some stick now.' Apart from 'Come on, Holmesy, pull your bloody finger out' and other, similarly mild suggestions, the disdain, thank goodness, was contained. But I'm not kidding myself. I'm sure I got away with it and was forgiven my deficiencies only because I was local, a product of their parish, and therefore could do no wrong. Blood's thicker than water at Cardiff.

Intriguingly, most of the 'verbals' came from one side of the pitch, the North Enclosure. While the South Stand is relatively restrained by what might be described as the more formal elements of the club – the committee box, the Press box and debenture seating – the Enclosure is a real mix of Cardiff folk, who in many ways are the true fans, always there, come rain or snow or frost. This is where the players (and some of the alickadoos) prefer to watch when they're not playing. There's a camaraderie in the Enclosure, a lovely informal, bubbly sort of atmosphere which is rich in humour and banter, which can be rough and ready, coarse and as abrasive as sandpaper. Sometimes the game is only the backcloth to the gossip and chitchat among members of this club within a club. I love it over there because I can identify with everyone and, if it comes to it, can give back as good as I get. Some players, though, would rather dive into a shark-infested pool than pay the Enclosure a visit.

It all boils down, I suppose, to being accepted. Take, for instance, Alex Finlayson and Chris Webber, two very good players in their own right, but who always seemed to have trouble in being adopted by the Enclosure fans. Whether it was because of the way they played, what they did, the way they looked or dressed or combed their hair, nobody'll ever know. The peculiar chemistry between spectator and player just wasn't there when it came to Alex and Chris.

None of us will ever forget the really miserable time 'Webbs' suffered with one particular fan. No matter what he did, the fault-finding rogue would single him out, running up and down behind the barrier parallel to the Enclosure touchline, hurling abuse as he went. It became a ritual, match after match. Most of the time, Webbs, normally a placid guy, put up with it, but on one occasion he exploded. I've never seen him more angry as he raced to the touch-line. 'I'll kill the bastard,' he growled. He meant it too, and a few of us had to move in pretty quickly to restrain him from leaping over the barrier to sort out his abuser.

In similar circumstances, many players would have packed their bags and sought fresh fields and friendlier fans. It speaks volumes for Webbs's attitude and his regard for club that he's still there, even though his playing services are now required more by the Rags, the second team, than by the first XV.

I don't want to suggest that outsiders are never made welcome at Cardiff. Indeed, of all Welsh clubs, they are probably the most cosmopolitan. At Cardiff a player's a player, whatever his nationality, colour or creed, and provided he's good enough, of course, he'll be accepted and given the chance to play. This has always been club policy and in these days of 'have boots, will travel', more and more non-locals are likely to swell the ranks. It is a policy I wholeheartedly endorse.

Scottie and Gareth Davies are prime examples of players who as non-Cardiff men had to 'prove' themselves to the enclosure fans, and did so handsomely. Both are now almost as much Cardiffian as I am. The only trouble they had was picking up the local accent. Both tried very hard to master Kar-diff, but even private tuition from Stan Bowes (which was costly in terms of Brain's Dark) and Frank Hennessy didn't seem to help. They still talk funny, like.

Scottie earned his acceptance the hard way. No one doubted his playing ability, but some doubted the Englishman's capability to survive on a club circuit which was somewhat more arduous than he had experienced at St Luke's College and Rosslyn Park. Within a season all scepticism had vanished as dramatically as the pits in the Rhondda. From Aberavon to Pontypool, Ebbw Vale to Neath, he not only survived the inevitable 'welcome to Welsh rugby' encounters – a test of anyone's durability – but he earned respect for being able to hand out just as good as he got. When he showed he could also outdrink every member of the first team, we knew we'd never get rid of him. Eventually, they even made him captain.

We had to lay the law down with Gareth Davies. Being a West Walian, a Tumble boy and that, he was fluent in Welsh, see. Now Cardiff isn't exactly a hotbed of Cymdeithas yr Iaith, and whenever another Welsh-speaker came to the club, Gareth would immediately adopt him like a lost brother. Off they'd go, into a corner, with their iachi das and their duw, duw bachs, leaving the rest of us to cluck among ourselves and wonder what the devil they were talking about. We'd try to get their attention. 'It's your round!' we'd roar, in English . . . Kar-diff English, which is only a *bit* different. Made no difference. They'd merely shrug, pretending they didn't understand a word, and carry on with a discussion of a feature they'd read in *Y Cymro* or something interesting they'd seen on Sianel Pedwar. It was bad for team morale, we said; it had to stop. It did eventually. And, would you believe it, like Scottie, Gareth got the captaincy of Cardiff as well!

11

Cardiff Matches

When Paul Rees, of the *Western Mail*, obligingly compiled details of my ten years at Cardiff RFC, I expected at best they would serve as reminders of events and matches which might have faded from memory. I have never been much interested in statistics, and I looked forward with a mixture of fascination and anxiety to the fruits of Paul's labours. How would the record shape up? Would the facts reveal something I had overlooked? Was I in for any surprises?

Surprise there most certainly was, the biggest one concerning Cardiff's matches against English clubs. I had this vague and comforting notion that in matches against English opposition in which I played, Cardiff had done reasonably well. I knew instinctively, for instance, we'd won more than we lost. The actual record didn't take my breath away, but certainly it gave me pause for thought.

Excluding the Barbarians, who are not English in the accepted sense, I played for Cardiff against English clubs on fifty-five occasions; and it was pleasant to be reminded that on only two occasions was I on the losing side, against Bath and Coventry.

It would be silly not to admit I take some pride in this achievement, because it gives a fair indication of the strength of Cardiff over the years and the success they obtained during my career with them. That said, however, the bare figures are in some ways misleading for Cardiff have been stretched and tested by English clubs to a much greater extent than the record suggests.

It's very important to realise the advantages the Welsh clubs enjoy. In the first place, most of the senior clubs in Wales play within a relatively small area, a sort of coastal band ten miles wide and no more than sixty miles long. They also play each other regularly, often twice a week. There is a lot of local rivalry and this makes for very fierce competition between the clubs, which is sustained throughout the season. You just don't have an easy match in Wales. Welsh players become accustomed to pressure and that is very important. In England, the set-up is altogether different. The senior clubs are so widely distributed that inevitably they have to play many 'soft' fixtures between the top confrontations. The competition is therefore not sustained and the players often find it difficult to raise their game. I don't think Welsh players are *better* than their English counterparts in terms of skill or commitment, but the best English players are distributed among so many more clubs. We have the edge on the English in club matches because we play and are more accustomed to matches of high competitive quality. It is as simple as that. You'd never survive on the Welsh circuit with the philosophy: 'It's only a game.'

There are, of course, exceptions to the rule. In recent years, for instance, Leicester and Bath have concentrated on improving their standards. They not only encourage top players to join them, but they plan their fixtures to ensure as much competition as possible. This undoubtedly improves the competitive skills of their players and, all things being equal, they are equipped to give any Welsh club a run for its money. The days when an English club faced Cardiff on a hope and a prayer are long gone. Some of the hardest club games I've played have been against Leicester and Bath. Rest assured, at Cardiff we never took either of them for granted.

A case in point was our match at Bath in 1984. For them it was a tremendous occasion, and although it was a midweek match, I believe they had a record crowd, something like 16,000, supplying a big-game atmosphere which in my experience was unusual in England. We didn't travel there expecting an easy game, and knew we'd have to play at the top of our form to win. Bath had a lot of very good players, many of them of international standard. Also they *wanted* to win, and believed they could. This positive attitude paid dividends. They won by the odd couple of points in a highly competitive match, although we almost pulled it off.

Near the end we forced a scrum on their line. With our big and experienced pack, and from that position, I would have said it was odds-on that we'd score the winning try. But Laurie Prideaux, the referee, penalised me for putting the ball in crooked and the chance was gone. It was an incredible decision: I swear to this day that my feed was as straight as a die. With an all-international front row, who didn't need any of my help to win the scrum, why on earth would I want to cheat? That's something I've never done on the rugby field. I was pretty angry, and very disappointed with Laurie, whom I considered to be one of England's best referees. Still, if we had scored and won, it would have been an injustice to Bath. They had taken us to the cleaners.

I only played at Leicester once – and I fell foul of the referee there as well. Normally I take a referee's incompetence with a shrug. On this occasion I felt so outraged at the decisions that went against us in the first half that my anger and contempt were translated into an absolute determination to do something about it on my own. I really put myself about in the second half, the adrenalin was truly pumping. I scored a brace of tries and we won. Albert Francis reckoned it was the best game I'd ever played for Cardiff.

Even harder for Cardiff than either Leicester or Bath was the Coventry match at Coundon Road. Although Coventry are not the strong club they were when I started my first-class career, they are full of pride and commitment, particularly at home. I was never on a losing side against them at the Arms Park, but away it was a different story. In five matches in which I played at Coventry, we lost once and drew once, and on a couple of occasions we were rather fortunate to win. Coventry were always a very honest and hard-grafting side, although they did have their ups and downs. In 1979, I think, we scored over 70 points against them, and they had David Duckham in the side as well.

Cardiff had some highly entertaining encounters with clubs such as Harlequins and London Welsh, but although the standard of rugby was as high as the entertainment value, we always had the edge. I was on the winning side every time we played them, scoring six tries against each of them – so I have very happy memories of the 'Quins and the Welsh.

Another favourite opposing team for Cardiff was Bristol – a superb attacking side, home and away, always seeming to have big, athletic forwards. The truth was that Bristol-fashion suited Cardiff. We had the ability to adapt our style, and although we enjoyed playing a fifteen-man game, if need demanded we could switch to nine- or ten-man rugby. I played nine times against Bristol, and they managed to hold us to a draw just once. I still find it remarkable, however, that I was on the winning side for Cardiff every time that we played Bedford, Camborne, Cambridge University, Harlequins, Leicester, London Scottish, London Welsh, Moseley, Northampton, Orrell, Oxford University, St Ives, Wasps and Waterloo.

Cardiff's annual match with the Barbarians was a special date in the calendar, and one to which we all looked forward. I enjoyed Baabaas as opponents not only because the rugby usually was of a high standard, but because I scored more tries (nine) against them than against any other club, English or Welsh. Coincidentally, the only time I lost against the Barbarians was when John Scott, then a Rosslyn Park player, scored a memorable try for them. He ran like a stag for 40 yards with Roger Lane, who's no slouch, and yours truly chasing him like whippets after a hare. We never made an inch on him and he came back from the try-line wearing the biggest grin I've seen on any player. He joined Cardiff soon afterwards – but he never scored a try like that for us.

As might be expected, Cardiff had a much more difficult time on the Welsh domestic front, none more so than against Pontypool. I feel qualified to judge the giants of Gwent rugby because I made more appearances against them than against any other club. In fifteen matches against Pontypool I was on a winning Cardiff team on six occasions, five of them at Pontypool Park, and I unhesitatingly award them the title of the side most difficult to beat. I relished these battles, home or away. In my time, Pontypool played a limited, New Zealand-type game, which was extremely difficult to counter. When on top form they were irresistible and although I generally had to count the bruises afterwards, there wasn't one match I didn't enjoy. Usually it was physical and rough, but rarely dirty, and I have a whole catalogue of memories of personal battles with their scrum-halves and loose-forwards. Pontypool always seemed to bring the best out of me. I can't pay them a bigger compliment than that.

Performance Against English Clubs

		Home				Away				Try Total
	M	W	D	L	Tries	W	D	L	Tries	
Bath	3	2	0	0	0	0	0	1	1	1
Bedford	2	1	0	0	1	1	0	0	0	1
Bristol	9	5	1	0	4	3	0	0	4	8
Camborne	1	–	–	–	–	1	0	0	0	0
Cambridge University	3	2	0	0	0	1	0	0	1	1
Coventry	9	4	0	0	6	3	1	1	1	7
Harlequins	7	4	0	0	3	3	0	0	3	6
Leicester	2	1	0	0	1	1	0	0	2	3
London Scottish	1	1	0	0	0	–	–	–	–	0
Moseley*	5	2	0	0	0	3	0	0	4	4
Northampton	7	3	0	0	4	4	0	0	4	8
Orrell	1	1	0	0	0	–	–	–	–	0
Oxford University	2	1	0	0	3	1	0	0	1	4
St Ives	1	–	–	–	–	1	0	0	1	1
Wasps	1	1	0	0	0	–	–	–	–	0
Waterloo	1	1	0	0	1	–	–	–	–	1
Barbarians	7	5	1	1	9	–	–	–	–	9
	62	34	2	1	32	22	1	2	22	54

*including 1 appearance as replacement

I played my first match for Cardiff against our oldest Welsh rivals, Newport, and was to play them on another nine occasions, never ending up on a losing side. There were times when Newport were every bit as good as Pontypool and, to be honest, we sometimes won when perhaps the scales of justice were tipped the wrong way.

Another club that gave Cardiff a lot of problems was Bridgend. They always seemed to have a good pack and lively, imaginative backs. In my time they were the only club, apart from Pontypool, to win more than once at the Arms Park, although strangely we had a much better record at the Brewery Field. My personal record against such clubs as Ebbw Vale and Newbridge is pretty good; but I always remember them as hard matches. There was tremendous commitment, and they were always looking to raise their game simply because they were playing Cardiff.

In the 1981–2 season, when we won the Championship and the Cup, we played a limited game. The following season we changed completely, didn't win anything and didn't enjoy anything. In 1984–5 I think we struck a nice balance, running the ball when we had a chance, or tightening up if the opposition were posing a threat. We had a very good season. I hope some of it will be related to the captaincy!

Over all, I'd like to think Cardiff was a popular club. A certain amount of envy existed among other clubs, because of our history and our ability to attract the top players. But we worked hard at establishing good relationships with other clubs off the field, and when we played clubs such as Swansea and Llanelli, there was always a good rapport between the players. Personally I liked Swansea. At St Helen's it's free beer and very good food. We tended to stay longer after matches there than anywhere else; and it was the same when they came to the Arms Park.

I cannot overlook the part Glamorgan Wanderers played in my career. I scored my 100th try for Cardiff against them, in 1984, and – not many people know this – I also played for them, once, in 1977. Cardiff were playing a World XV as part of the club's centenary, and with Gareth Edwards number-one choice and the Rags – our second XV – not playing I was sort of redundant that day. So when the Wanderers asked me to play against South Wales Police, I was delighted to say yes. It was a good match, and I enjoyed myself, except for the fact that I took a bad knock in the face. That night I went to the Centenary Dinner at Cardiff Castle wearing dinner jacket, black tie and black eye.

Performance Against Welsh Clubs

| | Home | | | | Away | | | | Try |
	M	W	D	L	Tries	W	D	L	Tries	Total
Aberavon	10	7	0	0	4	3	0	0	1	5
Bridgend	11	3	0	2	4	4	0	2	0	4
Cross Keys	1	–	–	–	–	1	0	0	0	0
Ebbw Vale	8	4	0	0	5	3	1	0	3	8
Glamorgan Wanderers	5	3	0	0	4	2	0	0	3	7
Llanelli	9	2	0	1	2	2	0	4	3	5
London Welsh*	8	3	0	0	3	4	0	0	3	6
Maesteg	2	1	0	0	0	1	0	0	0	0
Neath	11	7	0	0	3	2	0	2	1	4
Newbridge	4	0	0	1	0	3	0	0	2	2
Newport	10	5	0	0	3	5	0	0	1	4
Penarth	1	1	0	0	0	–	–	–	–	0
Pontypool†	15	1	2	2	2	5	0	4	1	3
Pontypridd	10	5	0	1	3	2	0	2	3	6
Swansea	8	4	0	0	3	1	0	3	1	4
	113	46	2	7	36	38	1	17	22	58

*including 1 abandoned home match

†including 1 abandoned away match

I got an even better shiner, though, in 1981, an important year for me. I plighted the troth. Susan took a little persuading, but she agreed that we'd get married on Easter Monday so that I could play on the previous Saturday against the Barbarians. It was a good arrangement because, although we were playing Harlequins on the Monday, a lot more of my pals would be able to get to the wedding that day. Everybody wanted to play against the Barbarians. Susan missed the match because she was involved in all the arrangements, so she hadn't a clue that I had had a bang in the eye until she watched me in a television interview later that night and saw my eye was black. She was horrified. Of course it didn't matter to me overmuch, but there were some hilarious scenes at the church with the boys ribbing me unmercifully as Susan and other members of the family tried to manipulate my 'bad' side away from the photographers. They failed. We don't get out the wedding album too often.

12

Other Players

During my career in rugby I was fortunate indeed to play with – and against – some of the best players of my generation. Of the hundreds who impressed me with their skill and ability, or made a mark on me – some literally – a handful stand out, for a variety of reasons. I remember them all, but some of them I call friends, not in a casual or flippant way, but in the real sense of the word.

One of these is certainly Swansea's Geoff Wheel. My respect for him as a player and regard for him as a man go very deep. If ever I were pressed to name a side in which I'd give anything to play, my pack would certainly include Geoffrey Arthur Derek Wheel. He was a tremendous forward, who didn't take up the game until he was twenty-one. Having waved goodbye to a football career, which included playing for Swansea's reserves, he was playing for Wales within two years of first handling a rugby ball.

'Wheel-o' was a rough-hewn oak of a man, fiercely competitive, brave and resilient on the field, but with a surprisingly gentle, almost boyish nature off it. He was a natural comic, too, with a wide repertory of off-the-cuff stories and jokes. Not being a master of repartee myself, I thoroughly enjoyed being in Geoff's company, marvelling at his easy-going attitude, in such contrast to his aggression and commitment on the field. He never shirked his responsibilities and often did more than his share. His reputation as a hothead on the field was misplaced, for most of the time his concentration was exclusively on doing his job. Some of his opponents may have possessed greater athletic skill, but few, including New Zealanders and Australians, had his all-round ability in maul, ruck and line-out.

I played with Geoff ten times for Wales and often had reason to be grateful for his powerful presence. I can hardly describe him as a guardian angel, but few other players gave me such a sense of total security and dependability. These qualities were reflected in his career for Wales, which I think gives him claims to be one of the great Welsh forwards of all time. First capped against Ireland in 1974, he was on a losing side only once in his first seventeen appearances – an incredible achievement by any standards. That defeat was against England in 1974, when Geoff played only part of the match anyway, as a replacement for my Cardiff colleague Ian Robinson, who had to come off because of injury. Geoff went on to play a total of thirty-two matches for Wales, playing alongside another top veteran, Allan Martin, twenty-eight times.

Such are the statistics which fashion heroes, but in a country like Wales, where hero-worship traditionally is focused on backs rather than on forwards, I've always thought Wheel's achievements received paltry acknowledgement both at the time and since. Perhaps this tribute will help redress the balance.

Wales arrived in Australia for the 1978 tour not only as European champions, but having lost only three times since Geoff was first picked. One of those was the aforementioned 1974 England match for which he could hardly be blamed, and the others against Scotland in 1975 and France in 1977. Was it coincidence that Geoff played in neither? Mike Roberts was preferred against Scotland and Geoff had to miss the France match because of suspension, having been sent off along with Willie Duggan in the Irish match.

The extent of Wheel's influence following the ill-fated Australian tour of 1978 (which I have discussed elsewhere) may also easily be overlooked. From then until he was no longer required (in 1982) Wales endured only six further defeats with Geoff in the side; and only on two of these occasions can it be said that they were beaten decisively – against Scotland in 1981 (when the pack were surprisingly outplayed) and against Ireland in 1982 when the Irish were without debate the better side.

The other four defeats, however, deserve more than a brief mention. The results themselves tell only part of the story. Fate could have been kinder to Geoff and Wales.

When we returned from Australia, subdued but still simmering from the misfortunes that were piled upon us on that injury-blitzed tour, we were given an early chance to redeem ourselves. Our opponents were New Zealand, at Cardiff, on 11 November, a date etched deep in personal memory because it was my first appearance in a Welsh jersey at home.

Geoff, too, had cause to remember it for another reason. Injustice wears many guises and poor Geoff was singled out for a transgression which cost Wales the match. For 79 minutes he did a wholehearted job deserving of credit and praise – there were many who considered it was his best game for Wales – and he contributed mightily to help establish that on the day we were superior to the All Blacks. We had all worked hard for one another, no one more than Geoff, and if ever a team had cause to celebrate a job well done it was for this match performance.

Instead, we lost 13–12, and Geoff Wheel, the lion of Arms Park, was refashioned a sacrificial lamb by the referee, Roger Quittenton, who alleged that an offence by him at the final line-out merited the award to New Zealand of a penalty kick. This gave them the chance in the dying moments to pull off the greatest robbery since the Great Train Hold-up.

Arguments and debate in Wales v New Zealand matches are hardly new. They started in the very first match between the two countries in 1905 and have continued unabated since. They are part of each country's folklore, as obligatory in the recounting of the matches as the twists and turns in an Agatha Christie plot.

And plot there was of a different nature in 1978, I have no reason to doubt, particularly as the chief perpetrators have since admitted to cunning and connivance. No team taking the rugby field can compare in thoroughness of physical and mental preparation and in strategic planning with the New Zealanders. They work out every possible contingency within a game-plan, endeavour to play to that plan, and react accordingly if something goes wrong. This approach to a match (which, incidentally, I profoundly admire) is one of the reasons that they are so difficult to beat, and is quite a contrast to the much more spontaneous, play-it-by-ear attitude adopted by other countries. A lot of British players have more than a sneaking admiration for this attention to detail, although perhaps not everyone will admit it.

Doubtless there were many who smiled wryly that the All Blacks, in this match, should even have contemplated a particular course of action in the eventuality of their being a few points adrift near the end.

Ironically, their cunning solution wasn't required. Andy Haden and Frank Oliver performed their theatrical dives out of the line-out to dupe the referee into thinking they had been barged out by unruly Welsh forwards. The All Blacks duly got a penalty, but in Mr Quittenton's judgement it was because Wheel had leaned into Oliver, which is the old chicken-and-egg syndrome, for there were lots of people – Geoff included – who contended it was the other way around.

'I didn't do anything, honestly,' Geoff declared afterwards. Knowing him, and respecting his sincerity, I believe him. Or put it another way: as the record stands, Geoff's version has to be more reliable than either that of the referee or of the dubiously motivated Haden and Oliver.

I am not trying to discredit the referee. It is likely that Roger made a genuine mistake, perhaps hastily reacting when faced with a frantic flurry of jumps, pushes, nudges – and dives – that made up that final, fateful line-out.

I don't think many referees cheat or are guilty of calculated bias. On the other hand, they are surely liable to make a mistake, to be as fallible as everyone else. So why shouldn't they admit it? Looking back over the evidence, I'm left with the unreserved opinion that it was referee error which cost us the game. It is on that decision, and as a referee, that Quittenton has to be judged. It wasn't the first time a blunder has happened on the rugby field. It won't be the last.

Frankly, I cannot add much fuel to the controversy. I was near to the incident but I can't honestly describe what happened. The fact that I was so close to the alleged infringement and didn't see anything untoward – except Haden and Oliver's Hollywood antics – is not exactly evidence one way or another. I was concentrating on getting the ball – hopeful that we'd win possession so that I could get it away to Gareth Davies as quickly as possible for him to hoof it away safely to touch. We were all aware, Welshmen and New Zealanders, that there were only a few moments left, and that this line-out could be the last action of the match. How wrong we were: victory and defeat were hanging on a very thin thread.

While I'm a little sceptical that international referees obey an unwritten law about NOT awarding a penalty near the end of a close match, unless the transgression is blatant, I have to say that I was nonplussed by Roger's action. His decision has to be examined against what had gone before. He had refereed the line-out all afternoon with a casual disregard for all infringements. As far as I can remember, he didn't give one penalty at any line-out until that last one. So by awarding that penalty against Wheel, Roger was guilty of inconsistency, if nothing else. It was a one-off, indefensible decision. Players respect referees for consistency and when they fail to display it referees shouldn't be surprised that they lose that respect.

Because of the arguments and the dispute, one other very important event in the match was all but neglected. Brian McKechnie, with tremendous pressure on him, and from a difficult angle, kicked a superb goal. What a kick. What a *coup de grâce*. Even though it was good fortune in the first place that gave him the chance to kill off Wales and join the ranks of All Blacks heroes, you still have to admire his technique and skill – the cool assassin from Southland, blast him!

The Fates seem to have conspired against Geoff Wheel in other ways. Just as sickening for him, I'm sure, was missing a Lions tour. There can't have been many players ruled out from becoming a Lion for medical reasons, certainly none for an alleged dodgy heart condition. Barred after being selected to go to New Zealand in 1977 was bad enough. When a second medical examination later proved the original findings wrong, Geoff's relief must have been tinged with a certain amount of bitterness.

I've had to cope with my own share of bad luck, but it doesn't begin to compare with the mishaps that have plagued Geoff's otherwise impeccable career.

Geoff, bless him, was like a rubber ball. He kept bouncing

back, and was still one of the best lock-forwards engaged in first-class rugby in Britain when he retired in 1984. His ticker is OK in every sense.

Apart from Charlie Faulkner's age, I suspect one of the best-kept secrets in rugby was the reason why Mike 'Spikey' Watkins decided, out of the blue, to give up the captaincy of Wales and international rugby in 1984 after just one season in a Welsh jersey. I believe I know, but I'm not telling. As a pal, Spikey wouldn't want me to. I have a feeling he'll 'reveal all' in his own good time.

It goes without saying that Spikey and I are close buddies – which I admit may seem surprising considering he plays for Cardiff's oldest rivals, Newport, or as Stan Bowes describes them 'those black and amber bastards'. Spikey used to play for Cardiff, though, and that's when I first got to know him. Our friendship developed both on and off the field, and he is one of those I miss most since I moved up to Yorkshire.

Let's be honest, a night out with Spikey is an event, something you never forget. There are a lot of pretenders to the rugby entertainers' throne, but he is the king. Les Dawson and Frank Carson have the knack of holding an audience in their hands. Spikey isn't far behind them in that respect, I promise. I'd even go so far as to suggest that if he ever gave up his burgeoning business career and took up comedy professionally, he'd more than knock 'em in the aisles. His humour is brash, flamboyant and natural, his repartee as swift as a cobra's strike and just as deadly. If someone in the audience has a 'go' at him, he'll be cut down pitilessly. Spikey could stand on a chair in a crowded rugby clubhouse and get everyone's attention within seconds. I know. I've seen him do it. Although much of his material is new or spontaneous, he can repeat the same joke over and over again and still get a laugh. I know. I've heard them all – and I roar every time.

I remember when we were guests of honour at a dinner in Manchester. Obviously we drove up together, a journey during which Spikey rehearsed his patter and I tried to smooth over the rough edges of the speech I was to give. My contribution was received with polite applause, but when Spikey followed me to the mike, predictably he brought the house down. They absolutely loved him. Trouble was the organisers had also commissioned a bona-fide comedian to follow Spikey. Suffice to say that the guests made an inevitable comparison. The comedian lost out. He ended up by having beer drenched over him.

Spikey's sense of fun is not confined to the banqueting room. On another occasion we were at a dinner in Bournemouth, and because of bad weather, snow and frost, Spikey was keen to get back so that he could be sure of playing for Newport the next day. I wasn't worried overmuch. I'd checked and found out that Cardiff had cancelled their match. Spikey was convinced Newport would play, however, and we set off. The conditions gradually worsened, but they didn't really concern us for we were both qualified with Heavy Goods Vehicle licences, which meant we knew how to cope. Spikey drove. Somewhere, miles from home and still in England, we hit a particularly bad patch and the car slewed into a ditch.

'Don't worry, boy. We'll still get home.' Spikey's optimism glowed. And, sure enough, the help we were praying for appeared within a few minutes. A farmer arrived from nowhere and Spikey talked him into pulling us out with a tractor. No sooner had the farmer done his good deed for the night than Spikey leaped out of the car, unhitched the chain, raced back to the wheel and roared away into the blackness, leaving the farmer standing wide-eyed in the snow.

'Why did you do that?' I asked innocently.

'He probably would have wanted a drink for his trouble,' Spikey replied.

One of the best tours I ever went on was with Cardiff to Zimbabwe in 1981 – and Spikey came too. That was a guarantee that the off-the-field entertainment would be of a high order. So it was, particularly when, to his horror, Spikey found he had lost his boots, a battered but much beloved pair. 'What am I going to do?' he roared, half-accusing the rest of the players of nicking his prized possessions. Only one other Cardiff player on the trip wore same-sized boots – Spikey's mortal enemy, Alan Phillips. There's been a lot of speculation as to the cause of the animosity between the two. My feeling is that they were temperamentally unsuited. They were in competition for the hooking job at Cardiff and each was convinced he was better than the other. I reserve judgement on that, and it needs only to be said that both were good enough to play for their country.

'Why don't you ask to borrow Alan's boots?' someone suggested to Spikey. We waited with bated breath for the expected angry dismissal of such an absurd suggestion. Surprise, surprise, Spikey agreed it was the only solution. He approached Alan cautiously. We all waited for the explosion. It didn't come. Alan responded: 'Yes, all right, but they're probably too fast for you!' If there wasn't going to be an argument at least he could have a sly dig at his old rival. Spikey therefore wore Phillips's boots, but after the match, in the team hotel, one of the players enquired when he was going to return them. Spikey gave his answer. He threw them out of the window.

There is, though, another side to Spikey. For someone who lacked a formal education, he is incredibly knowledgeable. He sucks in facts like a sponge, and seems able to talk on any subject. Not only sharp as a tack in every sense, he exudes enthusiasm, and among other things he is passionately fond of his birthplace, and the people, of the Western Valley in Gwent. His Welshness sometimes borders on an obsession. He runs Ray Gravell pretty close in that respect. Spikey has a beautiful house, tastefully furnished, and likes nothing better than entertaining his friends there: the privileges of a self-made man. There is more, of course. He was also a very fine rugby player, and one of the most wholehearted captains I've played under. He had a forte for getting the best out of his fellow players. That's why the selectors brought him into the Welsh side, and he didn't disappoint them. Down at Newport, they think him one of the best captains they've ever had.

His international career, as we know, was brief, almost an afterthought; and, truth to tell, that honour came when his best playing days were over. For years he was regarded by many of his peers as number one in Wales but because of a transgression off the park he was denied the opportunity of proving it. The WRU sometimes can be very harsh and unforgiving. Maybe that was the saddest aspect of the career of this happy-go-lucky guy.

When I look at some of the genuine characters in the game, Steve Smith, the England scrum-half, stands high on the list. He was one of the most bubbly, chatty guys I've met in rugby, and very good company off the field. Smithy, I reckon, was the master chatterbox. He went around with a perpetual grin. For Smithy, life was meant to be lived – not a bad philosophy.

As a player, he had his limitations. Nevertheless, he was strong and determined: and I have to admit he was the most difficult scrum-half I ever played against. He was, not to put too fine a point on it, a bloody nuisance, always trying to make life difficult for you. He aimed to frustrate you in every way, niggling and chirping away incessantly. 'Come on, Holmesy, you're not that good,' or sneeringly, 'Is that the best you can do?'

It was out-and-out gamesmanship – anything to put you off your game. A perfectly legitimate exercise. You'd have to be daft to fall for it – but you do, of course. I didn't play against him often, but it was always hard work, and I was glad to hear the final whistle, when we'd shake hands and tell each other 'well done'. I remember once having a go at him. Out of pure frustration, I let go a right hand. I missed. Smithy smiled. I don't know whether it was scorn or relief. But no matter how our particular confrontation went, we always sought each other out after the match. You couldn't help but like him.

One of the strengths of Welsh rugby is the depth of quality players. Every week you come up against a player who may not be in international class, but who is so good, so hard, that you wonder why the selectors overlooked him. Roger Powell, the Newport flanker, is someone in that category. We nicknamed him 'Doormat' because he was always on the floor, durable and brave enough to take the kind of punishment that his role entailed. He was also extremely competitive, a full-blooded tackler and an 80-minute player, qualities which earned him a reputation as a scourge of fly-halves.

When Cardiff played Newport he often made Gareth Davies his prime target, chivvying and threatening him to try to put him off his game. A cool customer, though, was Gareth. Usually he shrugged off the verbal intimidation and sensibly stepped up a gear whenever Roger homed in on him. If anyone wondered why Gareth's passing and kicking were always a bit sharper against Newport than against any other side, the threatening presence of Roger was probably the reason. The physical contest between the two of them was fascinating, although many of the other players found it a bit boring to hear them chirping away at each other like a couple of impatient bluetits.

I remember getting embroiled in their private conflict only once, when we played at Rodney Parade in 1985. Although Roger and I are pretty pally, on this occasion he switched his attentions to me – probably because Gareth wasn't playing. He threw a punch and I'm sorry to admit I reacted. Of course, it was the usual rugby punch-up, more bluster and threat than blood or bruises. Like a couple of fairground wrestlers, we ended up on the ground, grappling and struggling. I think I won on pinfalls. Our private battle continued largely unobserved. No one took the slightest interest in us, not even the referee, a Frenchman, who gave us a disdainful glance, turned his back, and carried on with his other, more important duties following the play, which by now had moved some considerable distance away. Both a little red-faced, Roger and I eventually got to our feet and shambled after everyone like a couple of schoolboys who'd been caught smoking behind the bike shed. We had a good laugh about the incident afterwards over a pint.

I have already mentioned John Scott, the England No. 8, who was a playing colleague of mine at Cardiff for many years. Our contretemps in the Twickenham international of 1980 gave rise to some daft rumours about our relationship: how we despised each other and how we were always pouring scorn on the other's playing ability. In fact, we got on very well, on and off the field. Perhaps the rumours got about because of our banter, which was intended specifically for the amusement of our fellow players at Cardiff. For instance, I used to rib him unmercifully about his line-out play and the 'rubbish' ball that he palmed down to me. In response he'd have a go at my passing.

'You know, Ombre,' he'd say scathingly, 'there's only one slower service than yours in Wales – and that's down at Pepe's.'

117

This was a popular eating-house in Caroline Street, notorious for the long wait customers endured before they were served. Naïvely, I asked Gareth Davies whether the comparison was justified. 'No, of course not,' he replied witheringly. 'Pepe's is much better. Scottie obviously hasn't been there for some time.'

Scottie will have to think up something new now, and find another victim for his caustic humour; both Pepe's and I have shut up shop in Cardiff. But I still see him. Occasionally he pops up to see me playing for Bradford Northern and I always seek him out whenever I pay a visit to Cardiff. Funny thing for so-called enemies to do, isn't it?

Rugby, as I've said, is about meeting people and making friendships. One player for whom I had particular respect was Seamus Oliver Campbell, as genuine and likeable a guy as you could wish to meet.

I got on well with Ollie, I suppose, because I saw in him one of my own characteristics, that of being generally quiet and undemonstrative. I don't think I have ever heard him utter a disparaging word against anyone. He has a lovely, equable nature and a wonderfully placid attitude to life. When I signed for Bradford Northern I had hundreds of good-luck messages and cards, from Cardiff and the WRU, from players, colleagues and friends, and from people I didn't even know. It doesn't really need to be said, but I appreciated every one of them. The card that I treasured above all, though, came from Ollie, partly because of its novelty and partly because I didn't expect it. It was designed in the shape of a shamrock, and it said: 'Hope this clover will bring you a bit of the luck of the Irish! Take it easy on those Rugby League softies too! All the best. Ollie C.'

Towards the end of his career Ollie had more than his share of injuries, and when eventually he gave up the struggle against his misfortune, the game lost a great character and a far, far better player than anyone gave him credit for. Ollie rewrote the record books with his kicking, and most people will remember him just for that. But it does him less than justice, for he was a highly gifted player with the ball in hand, an accurate and timely passer who could get his line moving sweetly. He didn't attempt a break very often, but when he did he could tear a defence to shreds. His style of play was uncannily similar to that of Gareth Davies, and he wasn't far behind Maj with line-kicking. Nothing seemed to ruffle him, and his assurance in everything he did gave his fellow players a tremendous sense of confidence. Ireland was always a very good side when he was in it – not only because he could kick them to victory. I became friendly with a lot of the Irish lads over the years, but my favourite Paddy of them all was, as they say over there, your man, Ollie Campbell.

A good few of my friends outside Cardiff can be found at Pontypool, which, during my time in first-class rugby, supplied some great players for Wales and the Lions. The Pontypool front row was rightly famous and even now I wonder at their collective dedication. They were all great characters, different as chalk from cheese, but with the same unbending resilience. Charlie Faulkner dropped out of action first, but Graham Price, incredibly, is still playing top-class rugby after three Lions tours. I don't know where Pricey gets his batteries from, but I wouldn't mind some of the same. Had he not been so dedicated to Pooler I feel sure he could have made it in Rugby League, and few Rugby Union forwards are equipped to do that. He was not only strong and committed, but he was an athletic prop, who could run and handle like a flanker. Gareth Davies tells me that the hardest tackle that he ever suffered was inflicted on him by Pricey – in a sevens match at Aberaeron.

Bobby Windsor obviously drinks at the same fountain of eternal youth. He was playing at the top level when I was only a callow teenager, and he is still at it, turning out occasionally for the second team. I reckon the only way to stop him is to shoot him, or for Pontypool to tie him down to a coaching contract. He can always go for a few tips to his old pal, Charlie, who has made a very good job of coaching Newport.

Jeff Squire and Eddie Butler are two other Pooler players for whom I have great respect. Jeff and I were very close for a time, seeing quite a bit of each other outside rugby. I always regarded him as a tremendous player and he trained very hard, both for Wales and the Lions, to keep himself at the top. Jeff played a lot of his rugby on the blind-side, but in my opinion (which I believe he shares) he was better-suited by No. 8. Eddie Butler was a play-anywhere forward, but for some reason which mystifies me and others who played with him for Wales, he was never accepted as a top-class performer by the media. He was a very good captain of Wales, too, and I think it was tragic that he was hounded out of the game by the critics. Maybe he talked too posh for them, I don't know. He has left teaching and has now been taken on by the BBC as a rugby programme producer, which enables him to pop up now and then with some shrewd comments on the game. He'll be critical, but I bet you won't hear him knocking players.

One of my favourite rugby players was Dai Richards, the Swansea centre. As a player, one word summed him up – Class, with a capital C. Like Eddie Butler, he left the international scene far too early, probably because of his work commitments. When he was playing at the top of his form, Dai was one of the most exciting and dynamic players I've seen. I'm not knocking his ability as a fly-half, but he was a better centre, a position where his speed off the mark, reflexes and creative abilities were better-employed. Wales have a long tradition in producing high-class centres. Dai would have been in the top half-dozen of all time, in my view, for there was not one weakness in his game. He was great fun off the field, too, and thoroughly earned his nickname of Dennis the Menace. The rule was never to let Dai anywhere near a fire extinguisher or a soda siphon; and he was even worse when he allied himself to his impish henchman Gareth Davies.

Dai scored four tries in seventeen appearances for Wales, but unfortunately he'll be best remembered for one that he didn't score, against New Zealand in 1980. Didn't he get some stick for that! He intercepted and broke away, almost from the Wales try-line, but didn't make it to the All Blacks' line. Dai, like the rest of us, had been defending for about twenty minutes solid and we were absolutely knackered. When he raced away, it was a relief just to get the ball out of the 25-metre area. The rest of the Welsh team thanked him. The critics panned him. We live in a funny world.

Someone else who was not always favoured by the critics but

was popular among his fellow players was Elgan Rees, the Neath
wing. I call Elgan the gentleman's gentleman, and his ready
smile and good nature were loved by all. Neath had a gem in
him, as a player and as a servant of the club. At the latter end of
his career, he was a regular presence in the Welsh squad and
often he was there with no realistic chance of getting a cap. He
never complained or quit; he just turned up every time he was
invited, honoured that the selectors felt he could contribute. I
don't know if it's true, but I'll bet Elgan has been a great help in
the development of young Jonathan Davies at Neath. Jonathan
is a cocky little devil – I know. We worked together for the same
company in Cardiff.

I was also Jonathan's scrum-half and captain when he got his
first cap, against England in 1985, on the withdrawal of Gareth
Davies over the A. N. Other incident. He came up to me before
the game and asked me: 'What do you want me to do?' I smiled.
'Go out and play your own game,' I said. He did. He scored a try
and a dropped goal and we won. It didn't surprise me one bit.
Jonathan is just like Mark Ring (Ringo) – his confidence
overflows. He's not frightened of trying things or of making
mistakes. He may lose a few points but he'll win a hell of a lot of
matches, too. His potential is unlimited. Maybe one day I'll have
reason to boast that on my last appearance for Wales, against
Fiji, the man who played outside me was Jonathan, the little
genius from Trimsaran.

One of the advantages of playing a long time is that your
career encompasses many generations of players. On the one
hand, I go out of the game having played with Jonathan Davies.
On the other, I am proud to have been in the same team as Ray
Gravell, who was playing schoolboy rugby before Jonathan was
born.

Gravs is a man of many parts, but there was never any doubt as
to his nationality. I don't believe a Welshman has been born
more passionately fond of his country. In another age he'd have
been leading Owain Glyndywr's troops into battle or firing the
tollgates and the haylofts with the Hosts of Rebecca. Instead he
had to settle for defending his country's honour on the rugby
field, which he did with some panache. 'Come on, boys, let's go

and get 'em,' Gravs would exhort in the changing room, smacking a fist into his hand. Other times, just before kick-off he'd be singing his head off while sitting on the toilet. He really did fancy himself as a singer. He cut a disc once, and gave Susan a copy as a present. Nice tune. Pity about the voice, and the words. Welsh, of course. I've never understood it. On another occasion, when he was appearing in a Welsh-language programme on S4C, he implored the rest of the team to switch on and watch. At the next team meeting he came up to us, bouncy and enthusiastic, and enquired: 'Well, boys, what did you think of it?' 'Not bad,' we lied. We didn't want to tell him that most of us, being non-Welsh speakers, hadn't a clue what the programme was all about.

Something was always happening with Gravs. In the evening following Wales's First Test defeat against Australia in 1978, Gravs was drowning his sorrows along with the rest of us. His tipple in those days was what I call Navy deaf and dumb, and that's just how Gravs ended the night. As I was lurching off to bed I found him lying crashed out in the hotel foyer, half in, half out of the lift, with the door opening and closing on his head. Next morning, he tottered down to breakfast, looking absolutely ghastly. 'I've got this terrible headache, I don't know why,' he moaned. Oh, yes. I almost forgot. Ray Gravell also *played* for Wales: and what a good player he was, rangy, strong and much more subtle than his reputation as a crash-ball player indicated.

I'm often asked my opinion of opposition players. Many Welshmen don't seem able to accept that other nationalities can play this game of ours. They can and they do, very well. I've come to the conclusion that at top level there really isn't a great deal of difference in class or ability between one international player and another, whether he's English or Welsh, Scottish, Irish, New Zealander, French, South African or Aussie. Of course, I've played against some exceptional players, like Andy Irvine and John Rutherford of Scotland, Danie Gerber of South Africa, Fran Cotton and John Scott of England, and a whole host of Irish and French players. If I were pushed to award top spot, my vote would have to go to Dave Loveridge. There was so much that I admired about Dave's play; a really great player, the complete scrum-half. If I had the chance to be reincarnated, I'd want to come back with his skill and attitude.

At the highest level in the game, however, skill and commitment are not enough. Players must improve their fitness in every way possible, and although this necessarily means ploughing a lonely furrow, going out running on dark, wet nights, or whipping your body to the point of exhaustion in a gym, there is no other solution. Success doesn't come easy in rugby, and anyone who thinks otherwise should abandon ambitions to play at the top level. There are plenty of opportunities to play lower down the scale for those not prepared to ask 100 per cent of themselves.

Certain players need a little spur or even a dig in the ribs to do something for themselves. A case in point is Alun Donovan, who was capped for Wales from Swansea but is now a regular at Cardiff. I got to know him well when we both toured Australia with Wales in 1978, and although he was badly injured on that tour I saw enough of him to realise what an accomplished player he was. I derive great satisfaction that Donny has done so well at Cardiff, for no other reason than that I was responsible for bringing him to the club. I'll admit it was poaching. No other word for it.

Gareth Davies and I went along to watch Swansea play Pontypool in the Welsh Cup Final in 1983. We wandered into the bar before kick-off and there, much to my surprise, his moustache wet with ale, was Donny. My natural reaction was that he must have been injured; nobody would want to miss the Cup Final. 'Hello, Donny,' I said. 'Hard luck. Injured, are you?' 'No,' he replied mournfully. 'I've not been picked. They're playing Tony Swift in the centre.' 'You've got to be joking.' My reaction was spontaneous. Swifty was a good player, an England international, but he was wing and never in my opinion a centre. Not for me, however, to criticise Swansea selection. The Jacks don't need me to help them make a mess of things. Quickly I changed the direction of the conversation. 'I tell you what, Donny. We're desperate for a centre at Cardiff. Why don't you think about joining us?' Thus, by accident, and a touch of Holmes connivance, Alun Donovan became a Cardiff player. He hasn't regretted the move, but I'll bet Swansea have. They lost a very good player.

Donny was a tremendous influence in Mark Ring's development, sometimes to his own detriment. If you could criticise him, it was that he was too unselfish. I've even seen him giving a scoring pass over the try-line. Perhaps he lacked self-confidence, which with his speed and ability should not have been a problem. Yet, for all that, Donny did a good job at Cardiff. He was solid, reliable and consistent. You can't ask more of any player.

Another recruit from Swansea was Gareth Roberts, and like Donny he was a great acquisition for Cardiff. It was not long before he was rechristened. As he was one of the few players in the club with even less hair than myself, he soon became Ming, the Meanest Man in the World, after the cartoon character. He earned his nickname not because of his attitude on the field – for he is a very competitive player – but because of his slowness in getting to the bar. Not only was Ming lethargic in ordering a round of drinks, he didn't do so very often either. Fortunately, that was the only complaint that could be levelled at him. He came to the Arms Park in 1984, basically because Mark Davies had been appointed captain at Swansea. Ming, who'd played a record twenty-one times for Welsh Schools, realised that this would necessarily limit his appearances, and with his sights set on winning a Welsh cap, he said farewell to St Helen's, although he kept his job in Swansea as a pharmacist. To say his arrival at Cardiff was timely is an understatement. The previous season we had operated with left and right flankers, but this system somewhat inhibited the way we wanted to play. A fast, specialised open-side like Gareth solved the problem, and his presence added another dimension to our play. We had a tremendous season in 1984–5 and Ming had a lot to do with that success. I used to have a yard or two on all the Cardiff forwards – until Gareth arrived. He was a bit sharp, I can tell you, and when he went I had some trouble keeping up with him. The rest of the boys were delighted that he won his first cap from Cardiff, and even more so when he scored a try on his second appearance, against England. Deep down, Ming is a Swansea lad and always will be, although he'll probably claim shared allegiance with

Pontlliw, his birthplace, and Pontarddulais, his previous club. Just being able to pronounce those two names means Gareth had to be a Welsh-speaker.

No such split loyalties applied to Gerald Cordle. Like me, he's Cardiff through and through: a Docks boy, and as dark as Brain's stout. Gerald was the best athlete in the club during my time, and a fine runner, with a beautifully relaxed style. He made it look so easy. In truth, Gerald had to work very hard on his game, because he was not a natural rugby player. He also had to work hard to please the Cardiff supporters. They loved him when he was running in the tries. But when he began to drop his passes, they were less than charitable. Unkindly, he became known as Teflon.

Two Cardiff players who earned my respect, in terms of loyalty to the club, were Bobby Larkin and Owen Golding. Both were blind-side flankers and, although Larks often got a game at No. 8, they both missed out because they were competing for the same position. The selectors had to adopt a horses-for-courses policy regarding the two of them, which was simply a compromise. Cardiff didn't want to lose either of them. At one time or another Larks and Owen were entitled to seek fresh pastures – Bridgend, for instance, were very keen for Larks to play for them – and it says much for the boys' attitude that they stayed. Larks, a rugged farmer, must hold the Cardiff record for not ever going off for an injury. I can't think of an occasion when he was knocked about so badly that he needed to leave the pitch; and he certainly got his share of punishment. He suffered so many cuts and splits on his head that he was automatically nicknamed Money-box.

Bobby Norster, in my view the nearest we have in Britain to the kind of big athletic forward so common in the southern hemisphere, looks certain to be Wales's No. 1 line-out jumper for years to come. I reckon he's been Britain's best since 1982 and it was a tragedy that he was injured with the Lions in New Zealand in 1983, when he was only twenty-six, because it lost him the opportunity of proving himself among the best in the world. I've played scrum-half to many good locks and Bobby was by far the best at giving me line-out ball. He could jump and take two-handed, and he rarely missed me with palm-downs. A lot of credit for Bobby's immaculate line-out jumping at Cardiff must go to Alan Phillips, whose throwing in was nearly always spot-on. It is interesting that when Norster sometimes played for Wales with less than good line-out feeders, he had to struggle to get his own ball. There's a moral there somewhere.

If ever I had to coach forwards, I'd make sure that they spent a lot of time practising line-out drill – particularly throwing in. I'd have the feeder practising his throws until he was able to hit a 5p piece on a basketball net ten yards away – every time. I'm surprised how little attention seems to be paid to this area of the game, for when it's wrong, it not only makes a scrum-half's life difficult but affects the whole team effort.

Norster had something of a superstition: he insisted on being the last man to leave the changing-rooms before kick-off. As I liked to be last but one out, there used to be, shall we say, a little bit of jostling between us. There were times when the rest of the side were out, warming up and wondering where the devil Bobby and I were. Bobby was bigger than me, so he always had the final word. Often he'd find some delaying excuse like tightening his shoe-laces or adjusting his head-band in the mirror. And eventually out he would trot, sometimes pushing me in front of him.

The Pontypool front row, as I've said, have a special place in Welsh rugby history and their legendary exploits will be remembered long after the words of the song that Max Boyce devoted to them are forgotten. But when Graham Price, Bobby Windsor and Charlie Faulkner finally had to apply for their bus passes, I don't think anyone would argue that their successors in all respects were the lads from Cardiff. It is fascinating to reflect on the battle these two front rows would have had if they had faced each other in their prime. I'm prejudiced, of course, but I might have had 10p on Ian Eidman, Alan Phillips and Jeff Whitefoot. On the other hand, I'd probably have to keep my money to phone for an ambulance.

The Cardiff boys, as a trio, did not come on the scene until Charlie and then Bobby departed to leave Pricey to carry the flag. The gradual all-round improvement of Cardiff's two

'orrible twins, Ivor and Jeff, as we called Eidman and Whitefoot, was close to sensational. Both had to work very hard at
their game, but they became excellent scrummagers and were
the main reason why the Cardiff pack was respected by everyone
– Pontypool included. This is not to ignore the gaffer who
scrummed down between them. Alan Phillips was the boss,
that's for sure. There were a few murmurs of disagreement when
I selected the highly volatile Alan as my vice-captain, but I
didn't care. He had been a great servant of the club and
nominating him my deputy was my way of thanking him. Then
what does he go and do? He becomes so popular with players
and committee that he gets himself the captaincy two years in a
row, including winning the Cup. He has quietened down a
lot, with the responsibility and all that, and I'm told that at
last he accepts without a snarl the nickname given him by
Pablo Rees – Johnny No Legs. The rest of us had a bit more
respect. We called him Thumper. He liked that better. Don't
know why.

The Cardiff changing-room was always a forum for ideas. All the
players, senior and newcomers, were encouraged to air their
thoughts. Roger Beard, our coach, was no authoritarian and he
laid great emphasis on the exchange of views. He *wanted* the
players to respond, to feel part of the coaching policy, and
ultimately to play the game that they wanted to play. He felt that
being a good listener made him a better coach, and helped to
obtain the desired results. The system worked very well in my
time with Roger at the Arms Park, so well that he needed to
employ the metaphorical whip only when he felt that the players
had not given full commitment in a match. The trouble with such
a democratic coaching policy, however, was that certain players
over-indulged themselves. Ringo was one of these.
  Most players would occasionally submit an idea for a move,
usually in the light of a recent match experience. Mark Ring
(Ringo) was different. He used to drive Roger to distraction
with a flurry of suggestions at every training session – 'Why
don't we try this?' or 'Wouldn't it be better if we did that?'
Roger was polite and attentive but often he found himself

cornered, ducking under a salvo of Ringo's ideas for midfield moves. Let me say that a lot of Ringo's ideas were innovative and based on good thinking – I used to believe he spent the whole of his working day conjuring them up – but, conversely, some were so way out that we'd have had to employ a computer to translate them from theory into practice. How Roger contained himself, I don't know. There were times when I thought he'd explode and Ringo would find himself lifted bodily by our large, powerful and hairy coach and thrown over the Arms Park bank into the River Taff.

Ringo's off-the-field theories were not the only cause of Roger's impatience. Whereas often he was absolutely brilliant in a match, there were times when he committed such outrageous acts that no one, himself included, knew what was happening. I think Ringo had this notion that he was out on the park with fourteen players and that all the rest of us had to do was to go along with his thinking and his actions. It rarely happened like that. When it worked it was good. When it went wrong it could be disaster.

A case in point was during a match against Aberavon while I was captain of Cardiff. Against Aberavon you do *not* take liberties, and if you expect to win you have to adhere to the basics. There was extra pressure, because the match was being televised for showing on 'Rugby Wales' the next day. Well, the match was not very old when Ringo performed his peculiar version of the miss move. His passing could be on the casual side at the best of times, but this one was a shocker, missing every Cardiff player and going straight into the hands of the Aberavon wing who gratefully accepted it and raced the length of the field for a try under the sticks. The conversion went over and we were six points down. I was furious, but as captain I made it a policy never to dress down anyone on the field. Instead I gave Ringo the Big Stare, which implied: 'What the hell do you think you're doing?' A lot of players might have skulked away or mumbled an apology. Not Ringo. Quick as a flash he responded to my glower. 'Ombre, do you think they'll edit out that pass tomorrow?' I almost fell over with laughter.

On another occasion, Ringo didn't have a very good game and

Roger, normally cool and self-possessed, charged into the changing-room. He was furious and he let Ringo know it. Ringo took it all in his stride, as calm as you like, and when Roger had finished he shook his head and said: 'Ah, well, Roj, that's entertainment, isn't it?' He gave the impression he didn't care a hoot, although my view is that deep down Mark Ring cared a great deal. He was a perfectionist, an idealist even, and his defence when things went wrong was an outward expression of nonchalance.

If there was one player capable of controlling Ringo, it was Alun Donovan, the quiet man of the Cardiff back division. Donny worked well with our erratic midfield genius, curbing his impulsiveness and restraining his brashness with a word or a warning. Donny's steadiness and overall perception gave Cardiff – and Ringo – a discipline it needed.

It was a great tragedy, of course, when Ringo suffered a terrible leg injury in 1985. A lot of people thought he'd never play again. When the surgeons had finished with him he looked like a survivor of a battle with Jaws, his leg criss-crossed with hundreds of stitches and scars. It didn't surprise me that he fought his way back to fitness and resumed duties for Cardiff. Then, nothing about Ringo surprises me. I'm sure when he's fully recovered, he'll show everyone that he is a world-class centre. The game needs his exciting and exuberant talent.

In my time at Cardiff, one of the real characters there was Paul 'Pablo' Rees, our full-back. Pablo and I went to the same school, Bishop Hannon, and although he was a year older we followed similar paths, playing together for Cardiff Youth and Welsh Youth, the Rags and eventually the first XV. Pablo certainly had the wanderlust. When he was doubtful of a first-XV place, or at least wasn't getting many opportunities, he joined Ebbw Vale and after two seasons at Eugene Cross Park he moved south, to Newport. We all knew that his heart was in Cardiff, and eventually he rejoined the club and became our regular first-team full-back. His right to hold down the job was unquestioned. A big, strapping fellow, well over 6 feet, Pablo was well-nigh unstoppable when he launched himself into the three-quarter line. His greatest quality, though, was his assurance and coolness under the high ball. We called him the Rock of Gibraltar. At his best, there are not many better full-backs in the game. He was unlucky not to have featured in selection for Wales, although he won a B cap.

Pablo was tremendously popular with the players at Cardiff. A funny guy, like Geoff Wheel, who could crack a joke and take one. He loved being the centre of attention, and didn't mind one bit when the rest of the lads 'had a go' at him. He was notorious for his *faux pas*, which led inevitably to the boys querying the intelligence of the products of Bishop Hannon. 'They must have turned out some real dimwits, that school.' Neither Pablo nor I was impressed by that piece of logic, but Pablo was enshrined as a member of what the boys called the Bishop Hannon Hand-biter's Club whenever a teacher asked him a question. Pablo's reaction was to bite his hand and yell 'Aargh!' It became a cult story within the club and was told over and over again. It never failed to get a laugh.

I have my own favourite story of the many that concerned Pablo, who incidentally was not as daft as the boys tried to make him out. Mad, yes, daft most certainly not. We were halfway through a club dinner when Ringo hastily got to his feet to leave the table. 'Where're you going?' enquired Pablo. 'I have to go. I've got to ring my girl-friend,' said Ringo. 'What on earth for?' Pablo was mystified. Ringo explained, 'Look, my girl-friend's a religious nut. I have to ring her to check that she's gone to church.' Pablo was baffled. 'WHAT are you talking about?' Further explanation was obviously needed. The rest of us sat there in eager anticipation. Ringo – who was always trying to get the better of Pablo, rarely with success – proceeded to tell Pablo of his girl-friend's extraordinary obsession. 'You know, she's absolutely incredible; next week she's off to Lourdes, would you believe?'

We all looked at Pablo. His mouth hung open. 'Lord's? Lord's? Don't tell me she plays cricket as well. Do she?' Exit Ringo, tears rolling down his face.

Part of the reason why Gareth Davies and I rarely missed training at Cardiff was that Pablo was always there as well. No matter what the weather, how cold or wet and miserable, or how low we felt, Pablo had the ability to make a dull, uninspiring training evening a joy. He was our cheer-leader and fun-maker, and I'm sure he made Roger Beard's job easier on such occasions.

It was not all training and playing at Cardiff. The social side was excellent, both at formal dinners (which players scoffed at but usually thoroughly enjoyed) and informal gatherings. Players' parties were always a bit special, and often highly original. There was one fancy-dress night, which was modelled on a cabaret from *Some Like It Hot*. Andrew Yeandle, one of our wings, and Huw Davies, the England international, were beautifully turned out – as demure young ladies. They played their part to the full, too, holding hands all night. This set the cynics among the players wondering. The rest of us knew the truth, though. Nothing gay about those two, that's for sure.

Since I went to Bradford, by the way, Pablo has moved on again from Cardiff. He's back at Newport. On the grapevine I was told he upped and went back to Rodney Parade when he discovered that Newport were planning a tour of Hawaii and Australia. Typical Pablo.

Another rumour that's come my way is that Adolf has been training too, which is a bit of a shock. Adrian Hadley loves every aspect of the game – except training. He reckons he is super-fit, and doesn't need to top up like the rest of us. He used to get away with it at Cardiff because, simply, he was one of the most brilliant players in the club. Fit or not, trained or not, Adolf was a superb player, with incalculable potential. As someone who believes Adolf will go on to become a truly great player – he's still only a youngster – I was a bit surprised when Wales decided that they didn't need him at the start of the 1987 Championship. A quiet, introspective sort, Adolf was a bit of a fringer like myself. For all that he was a good lad, respected and popular. He liked the joes and his dark, as we say in Cardiff.

Mark Ring is an altogether different type. Brash, bubbly and enthusiastic for everything. Ringo can hold his own with anyone in the chat stakes, although perhaps he tends to take himself a shade too seriously when it comes to discussing centre play. I think of him as one of the most exciting young players we've produced in Wales for years. In a word, he has flair. He is supremely confident in his own ability, and he has that precious quality of being able to destroy a defence in an instant. Some of the tries he scored for Cardiff were quite superb.

When I look back at my days – or, rather, nights – of training at Cardiff, I realise what a rich and varied experience it was. Before Roger Beard took over, the Cardiff coach was John 'Buck' Ryan. Buck was a disciplinarian and a great motivator. This, allied to an inherent bluntness and abrasiveness, won him respect if not many friendships in the club. Buck was another example of someone who, in his way, loved Cardiff and wanted the best for the club. Those were sufficient grounds for obtaining my regard and affection. He was a good coach, and he came to the club when it was undergoing a period of change, in the way we played and in the manner the club was run.

Buck, I understand, had some reservations about joining Cardiff. He told David Burcher, our centre, that he was uncertain how he'd cope in a club with so many top players. He was concerned, he told David, that the 'stars', as he called them, wouldn't knuckle down, for instance, to his strict training regimes. He was with Cardiff for two years, and I think he was pleasantly surprised to discover his fears were unfounded. Everyone responded, and his reward was to produce a succession of sides which not only believed in winning but achieved their success with high-grade rugby. Buck played an important role in building Cardiff into the club it is today. I for one will never underrate his contribution.

The cornerstone of Buck's coaching was fitness. One of his sessions I shall never forget. Nor will anyone else who had the misfortune to be part of it. We were branded for life; some players I know quiver at being reminded of it. The session was in South Africa, on tour. We had played reasonably well, and achieved some good results; but in Buck's view we had not shown sufficient commitment in our last but one match, in midweek, which we should have won. The final fixture of the tour was against Natal, one of the top provincial sides, and as we left for Durban, our last port of call, Buck promised us a really

132

hard last training stint. It was a five-hour bus journey to Durban, which was a killer, and we arrived at our hotel looking like wet rags, between two and three in the morning. 'You'll all be up in the morning, don't worry,' Buck threatened. We were. At 9 a.m. Buck made sure, jarring open bedroom doors, his eyes glinting like a galley slavemaster. We dragged ourselves down to the training ground. Talk of killing-fields. It was murder in Durban that day. I love training, but even I found it hard to cope with. I found out what the pain barrier really is. The boys moaned and cursed and tried every trick in the book to skulk away. Buck wasn't falling for any of it. I'm not sure how long the session lasted, one hour, two hours, three. It seemed like an eternity. It was like bashing your head against a wall – so marvellous when you stopped.

Two days later we played Natal. Buck's agony session worked. We played well and beat them comfortably, which in any circumstances was a landmark in the club's history. Buck came into the changing-room afterwards. 'Well done, lads,' he said. 'You played well.' We grinned. We knew what he meant.

When Roger Beard, with whom I developed a close friendship, took over from Buck, it took him a while to settle in, but eventually he became the most popular coach the club has had. He got on with players and committee alike and by guiding the club to two Schweppes Welsh Cup victories he even brought a smile to the face of the treasurer. Roger is one of those coaches who defies his pedigree. He was a prop-forward for the club for many years, and soon proved he knew a great deal about every aspect of the game. He never let himself be hamstrung by theoretical dogma, and his attitude was refreshing in other ways. He realised that with the quality players Cardiff possessed they didn't need much coaching in the strictest sense. His training sessions were prepared with this uppermost in his mind. He worked hard on communication and, although he rightly employed set routines, was always alive to new methods in order to maintain the players' interest. He saw his job, I think, as a moulder of men, of obtaining their support and encouraging them to perform to the peak of their ability. Each player was encouraged in loyalty to the club and to colleagues, and out of this stemmed an incredible team spirit. Let's face it, Roger *knew* the players; he'd grown up with a lot of them. When the rewards came – the Cup victories, the 'double' – he shared in the joy and satisfaction. He was one of us. In these days, when people seem to moan and carp and worry about professionalism creeping into the game, it seems to me worthwhile pointing out that Roger, for instance, never claimed one penny expenses in the first two years that he was coach at Cardiff. The club could have afforded to pay a king's ransom to a successful coach. Roger took his rewards in an altogether different way. Job satisfaction, plain and simple. Speaking of coaching, I should not forget Gary Samuel's role as assistant to Roger. Gary-Sam was an able adjutant, and his chief job, looking after the backs, was such a straightforward task that it was easy to overlook the huge amount of work he was committed to behind the scenes. Roger would swear by Gary-Sam. So would I.

Although I thought of Cardiff as better than most, there are two areas where coaching can improve. My own experience suggests that at senior level too little emphasis is placed on skill practice and a lot more needs to be done about the level of fitness. It's difficult to assess the role of the coach in such matters. What he most certainly shouldn't do is to denigrate skill sessions – such as players kicking to each other, practising drop-kicking and cross-kicks. A coach who thinks such activities a waste of time is failing to understand motivation. You shouldn't have to sweat pints to please the coach. Nevertheless, the relative lack of fitness is a widespread problem in British rugby. It is my contention that we are not as fit as our contemporaries in others parts of the world, and although a coach can help direct a player to get into better condition, in my view the individual's fitness is not his responsibility. The player himself should do a lot more. Recognising his fitness failings and doing something about it is a personal challenge, although in an amateur sport I realise this implies a clash of interests. How far can you go, or should you be expected to go, in a game invented entirely for fun?

When I put the film in the mental projector, I have to admit to a bit of sentimentality – those days at Cardiff were the best of my life, the most enjoyable, the most exhilarating. It was marvellous to be part of the set-up and the success, and to have friends who were good players. No rugbyman could ask for more.

13

Ringer

Over the years, I have been involved in a few highly charged and controversial encounters on the rugby field, but none to compare with the England–Wales match of 1980 at Twickenham. The match has earned notoriety largely because the Irish referee, David Burnett, sent off Paul Ringer for a high tackle on John Horton, England's fly-half. Both the crime and the punishment would have been highly questionable even in an ordinary match. To this day, people still get hot under the collar over the rights and wrongs of the Ringer incident: the Llanelli flanker was either made the arch-villain of the piece, or he was regarded as desperately unfortunate to have been singled out when other violence (some of it cynically premeditated) went unpunished. Either way, it will always be known as 'The Ringer Match', and Paul will ever be the condemned man, who has to live out his life knowing that there is nothing he can do or say which will diminish the disgrace.

Personally, I feel very sorry for Ringer, and I'm sure that many other players in that match, both English and Welsh, are equally sympathetic. The sending-off effectively ended his Rugby Union career. Although his sometimes crudely aggressive play did not earn him many admirers, not even his worst enemy would have wished that on him. Let's face it, there were not many players involved in the match who afterwards could put hand on heart and declare their innocence in a sometimes perilously physical encounter, in which the real culprit was the over-motivation of both teams. Many theories have been advanced as to why the teams went out on to the field set on a collision course, and probably there is a grain of truth in all of them. Some officials and players, who should have known better, and a couple of members of the Press, may have had a few sleepless nights for their part in sowing the seeds of a feud which was, to my knowledge, uncharacteristic of England–Wales matches. Usually, England v. Wales meetings are hard and demanding of both sides, and sometimes they are so exhausting and punishing that it takes weeks to make a full recovery. I'd also like to lay the myth about the Welsh having an inherent edge in competitiveness and ability. An Englishman is absolutely no different from a Welshman in being prepared to go to the limits of his skill, strength and endurance so that his side can win. 'Come on, boys, let's go out and beat them!' Add or change the stress, and a few expletives, and that kind of entreaty is common to both dressing-rooms before any international. The theme is the same; only the accent is different. Perhaps the difference, occasionally, is that a side which wants to win just a shade more than the opposition obtains victory. The vast majority of international matches are evenly balanced with perhaps one score, a flash of brilliance, or a bit of luck, making the difference between winning and losing. But if a player, any player, can't accept the idea of losing he shouldn't be playing the game in the first place. Of course, winning *is* important, but no game, whatever its imagined or real rewards, is worth the participation if ruthless or mindless violence is employed as the means to a victory. That's war, not sport.

I'm not suggesting the 1980 match was anywhere near that category. It was hard, really hard, and some players, stimulated by hyped-up pre-match pressure and red-hot passion during the eighty minutes, allowed the violent side of their nature to override common sense. The dividing line between physicality and dirty play is paper-thin. Only the best referees can judge the difference. I'm far from sure how many competence marks out of ten I'd award Mr Burnett, and I must say with all honesty, and considering what took place, that there may be some credibility in the view that he came to Twickenham briefed for a torrid affair. It is worth speculating that a much tougher approach from him in the first few minutes, rather than the few indulgent reprimands which he did issue, might have helped to produce one of the great internationals of all time.

When I think back on the match, and remember how some of my bruises were inflicted, the villains may well have outnumbered the angels; and even if Mr Burnett had possessed eyes in his backside he couldn't have hoped to keep pace with all that went on. It was extraordinary that some of the misdemeanours were committed by players of normally scrupulously fair and unblemished character.

On the other hand, there were some players who made tackles in that match who'd never tackled anyone before. Others ran and chased so hard that they could barely lift their feet to walk off at the final whistle. The RFU doctor, Leon Walkden, likened the English dressing-room to a casualty clearing station. He ought to have seen ours. Some of us looked as if we were in need of a priest, let alone a surgeon. The skill content, too, was overshadowed, which was the greatest injustice of all, for at times both sides produced some tremendous rugby at a break-neck pace. To my dying day, I shall applaud the seven-man Welsh pack. They were up against an English pack which had claims to be one of the best in their long history, and not only did the Welsh forwards hold them for most of the match, but occasionally outplayed them. That was spirit, character and guts, not villainy.

I'm told that England's captain, Bill Beaumont, poked his head through our changing-room door at the end and declared: 'Thanks and well done, boys – a tremendous game.' Personally I didn't hear it. But, knowing Bill, it would be no surprise.

On a personal note, the match should have been specially memorable for me for it was the first time that I'd played in an international at Twickenham. I was tingling with anticipation, and looking at the rest of the boys just before we trooped out I was acutely aware of being part of a charged-up atmosphere, a vibrant expectancy that I'd never experienced before or since. My Twickenham début was memorable all right; straight from the kick-off, at the first maul, I felt a huge, powerful hand grabbing me, fingers clawing at my eyes, and I thought I was going to have my head pulled off. I couldn't believe the identity of the culprit – no other than John Scott, the England No. 8 and my pal and colleague from Cardiff. Although Jeff Squire, my minder as it were, made one of his timely interventions and rebuked him with a couple of hefty clouts, personal retribution was a foregone conclusion. I got my chance soon after, at another fiercely contested maul.

We dug the ball out, Clive Williams tried to feed back to me, but for some obscure reason we were penalised. On the floor, with Clive, was Scottie. It was pure frustration, plus unthinking revenge, and I let the boot go. Just my luck – and Scottie's – that the full force of the kick caught another Cardiff player, Alan Phillips, who was grounded nearby. I'm not very proud of what I did, even if I'd argued a case for retaliation. It was a mistake, a petty and pathetic gesture in a match that was already boiling over.

Anyway I was determined to make amends, to play as well as I could, and to put everything into going for a try whenever we got close to the England line. Some chance. Scottie never gave me an inch, either flattening me with a full-blooded tackle, holding me up or pushing me wide so that I could never get a good thrust at the line. In the context of the match, I hate to say it, but Scottie was good, very good. Of course, he knew me and he knew my game, too well. It is no coincidence that although I scored nine international tries for Wales, not one of them was against England. Scottie, darn him, saw to that.

England, in the end, went on to win 9–8 and set themselves up for the Grand Slam. We scored two tries and Dusty Hare kicked three penalties. That is well known, part of history. Less well known is the fact that I actually cost Wales victory, or, more accurately, that the referee singled me out as the culprit. We were leading 8–6, and hanging on for dear life, when near the end Paul Dodge came down the middle like a train. I went in hard and brought Paul down, but unfortunately Geoff Wheel and Allan Martin, close behind me, piled in as well like a couple of runaway bullocks and in the process drove me over Dodge. Incredibly, the referee decided I was now on the wrong side of a ruck and that I had intentionally prevented the ball from being released. Penalty! It was sickening, unbelievable. No referee will ever make a more momentously wrong decision. England could hardly believe their luck. Up came Dusty Hare, good old reliable Dusty. Some of the English players couldn't even bear to look. Twickenham held its collective breath. Everyone knew it was a kick that would settle the match. Calmly, unhurriedly, Dusty stroked the ball between the sticks and it was all over.

Later, as the players crossed from the changing-rooms under the West Stand to the team bus, which was conveniently waiting for us in the adjoining car-park, you'd have thought we were going to a funeral. By now, an hour after the match, most of the spectators had gone home or were jockeying for pints in crowded local pubs, but there were quite a few stragglers around as we made the short walk to our transport.

'Hard luck, boys,' some of the Welshmen among them piped up consolingly, although it was obvious they were equally dejected. 'You were robbed' and 'Wait until next year, then we'll see who's best': typically Welsh, ever predisposed to dilute their grief with fragile optimism. Close by, other fans, obviously English, were rather less charitable. We had to endure a few choice remarks from these, and as we climbed aboard a noisier and more demonstrative group gathered. Their collective bravery had grown, too, and by the time we were all in our seats, they had assembled in hostile clusters around the bus. Taunts soon became insults, nasty ones, including the questioning of our fatherhood amid a flurry of Harvey Smiths. Regardless of the rights and wrongs of the match, none of us wanted this, nor did we think as players we deserved it. It was a sour climax to an unhappy afternoon, and not surprisingly we were pretty upset about it. Ray Gravell, who can't hide his feelings anyway, seemed to take the malice personally. He was seething, and was all for getting off the bus to discuss the matter with them. 'Let's go and sort them out,' he suggested, with undisguised anger. Wiser counsel prevailed. We stayed in the bus.

Later, after the wake, which was effectively disguised as the official dinner to both teams in the Hilton Hotel's chandeliered banqueting room, there was an understandable collective will to drown our sorrows. (The English players had a similar idea, but theirs was tinged with a different motive: the speeches at the banquet might have had something to do with it, too – they were terrible.) For the Welsh players, it proved a staggeringly painless exercise. By the end of a quite memorable, boozy night worthy of inclusion in the *Guinness Book of Records*, the afternoon's events were well and truly put to rest; players from both teams mingled sociably in little groups, laughing and joking with one another, and thoroughly enjoyed themselves.

It is often forgotten, or not realised, that hard or bitterly contested though a match might be, rugby players as a rule do not carry ill-feeling or animosity off the field. Respect and friendships do not wither and die just because of hot-headedness or over-reaction during a match. Once or twice earlier in the day, for instance, it might have been noticed that John Scott and I, in a manner of speaking, had called into question each other's toughness and self-control. But at night, at the teams' get-together, there we were, an Englishman and a Taff who had been close pals before the match and were still close pals, sharing a drink or two, and socialising as if we'd spent a sedate and leisurely afternoon together at a vicarage tea-party. We were not alone. Players from both sides mixed freely and amicably, and that's how it should be. The only squabbles usually stem from whose turn it is to get the drinks in. Even in that respect there was some comic relief, in the shape of Gareth Davies taking it upon himself to get behind the hotel bar to serve the drinks. May be a highly rated building society manager, our Gareth, but no great barman, definitely not. He dispensed the cheering liquid with the expertise of a kangaroo in boxing gloves. Allowing for spillage, as they say in the trade, everybody got doubles. And everyone got drunk. Later still, came sandwiches and coffee. And the argument.

As was our usual custom, Gareth and I shared a room. But this was one of those rare occasions when, courtesy of the WRU, girl-friends and wives accompanied players on the trip, although, probably out of diplomatic courtesy towards the un-marrieds, the ladies were allocated separate rooms. Now, you can't go to a hotel with your wife and then, come the witching hour, be expected to kiss her goodnight in the foyer and off you both go to separate bedrooms. Even allowing for alcoholic haze, such formality didn't make sense to any of us, and so, giving little thought to the sleeping arrangements, we agreed that the four of us, close friends anyway, would spend the night together in one room. Sort of happy families. The plan was sound enough; obviously one couple would have to spend the night on the floor. Just meant moving one of the mattresses from the bed. That's what started the debate.

'I'm not sleeping on the floor,' quoth I. Susan, who likes her creature comforts, beamed her agreement.

'Well, I can tell you, *I'm* in the bed,' said Gareth icily.

'You're bloody well not!' I responded. 'The bed's for the Holmeses, and that's that.'

'OVER MY DEAD BODY!' retorted Gareth. Helen was impressed with her man's brazen heroism, although she couldn't be absolutely sure whether he meant it or not. Knowing Helen, a practical lady if ever there was one, probably she was more concerned that his life-insurance premiums were up to date.

As the argument raged back and forth, the girls sat on the edge of the bed, watching like Wimbledon metronomes. Eventually, boredom set in, and like all the best friendly rows the matter was settled amicably. Logic won the day or, rather, the early morning. The girls shared the bed; Gareth and I had the floor.

'Told you, Holmesy boy, didn't I, that *you* wouldn't get the bed,' Gareth chuckled as we settled down to sleep. Always one for the last word, that so-and-so.

14

Wales Matches

When retracing a career of twenty-five appearances and seven years in the Welsh team, it is very easy to delude oneself that there was an inevitability about it all, that it was my destiny to be Wales's scrum-half. However, by probing one's memory a little more closely, and comparing the mental flash-backs with the facts, a rather different picture emerges. I realise how very lucky I was, and how much chance played a part in launching my international career.

In fact, I'm forced to the conclusion that my first cap, against Australia on 17 June 1978, the starting-point of the whole wonderful journey, was due more to accident and selectorial compromise than to destiny. It could easily have turned out differently.

The media flatteringly built me up as the natural successor to Gareth Edwards and predicted that Gareth Davies and I, as a pair, would automatically take over from Edwards and Phil Bennett. The truth is that no such certainty existed on either count. There were, for instance, other scrum-halves ahead of me and, regardless of what the pundits predicted, there was no natural heritage for Gareth or myself.

When the Welsh party left for Australia, it must be remembered that effectively I was selected as number-two scrum-half, behind Brynmor Williams, although he too was uncapped. I wouldn't even have been that, and perhaps not even on the tour, had Gareth Edwards not declared himself unavailable. Phil Bennett, another member of the 1978 Grand Slam side, was also a self-imposed absentee, which enabled Gareth Davies to move up a rung.

Another point is that I did not *expect* to be capped ahead of

Brynmor, senior to me in experience. Naturally, I hoped and prayed that I'd get the chance, but in my heart I knew it was unlikely. In the event, my scepticism was justified, for Brynmor was duly capped in the First Test at Brisbane. Although we lost, Brynmor played well and my chances of a cap in the Second Test seemed even more remote. But then things started going wrong for Wales, and ironically, right for me. A catastrophic catalogue of injuries wrecked selection plans, and with the Second Test at Sydney imminent, Wales had to reshuffle their depleted forces. It was compromise, pure and simple. J.P.R., the world's greatest full-back, was to play at flank as replacement for Terry Cobner; Alun Donovan, a centre, was chosen at full-back with Clive Davis at No. 8 and Stuart Lane at open-side. With such dramatic changes forced upon them, the only question left for the selectors to ponder over was scrum-half. Probably it was not an easy decision.

Brynmor, as I've said, played well in the First Test, so there was no reason to drop him on that account. I played well in the lead-up match, although we lost, against Australian Capital Territory. The dilemma for the selectors, however, was not to balance the experience or proven reliability of Brynmor against my good form and comparative inexperience, but to decide what tactics the cobbled-up Welsh team should employ. Necessity indicated a tight game, and this probably was the first factor which swayed the selection away from Brynmor to me. With our makeshift, and relatively small back row, my height and size could be important. No doubt the selectors also remembered that I had played very well earlier in the tour against Queensland and that it was the Queensland back row of Greg Cornelsen, Mark Loane and Tony Shaw which would be representing Australia. Another influence might have been the fact that Gareth and I were used to playing together at Cardiff, and as such might, if necessary, be able in combination to put the clamps on the Aussies. That was the theory – at least my version of it – and I was picked ahead of Brynmor.

When my name was read out I went up to him. 'Hard luck,' I said. 'I thought you played well in Brisbane and I was sure you'd be in.' Brynmor was obviously very disappointed, but he wished me well. Thus, at a stroke, my international career had started and his temporarily came to a close. He did not play again for Wales until 1981. Such were the twists of fate, which changed both our lives. To be honest, I was glad it was me and not Brynmor. But I still wonder, had the situation been reversed, whether he would have gone on to establish himself as Gareth Edwards's successor, leaving me out in the cold.

On that tour, incidentally, there was a little group of players very much categorised as the Wednesday team, and all uncapped – myself, Stuart Lane, John Richardson, Clive Davis, Alun Donovan and Spikey Watkins. None of us really believed we would make the Test side, for after all, with the exception of Edwards and Bennett, we would have had to displace players who'd won the Grand Slam. In the event, and because of the special circumstances of the tour, all of us in that little group of no-hopers made our Wales débuts, except for Spikey. His time, however, was to come. He went on to win his first cap as captain of Wales, a great double honour which was thoroughly deserved – although he had to wait six long years of frustration for it to happen. As I've said, nothing in rugby is certain.

There was one pleasant footnote to that tour. After the last match, J. J. Williams approached Gareth and me. 'I know we lost, boys, but I want to say well done to both of you. Don't worry about the result. I'm sure you're going to go on and play as many times together for Wales as Benny and Gareth.' We thanked him. It was a really nice gesture to two youngsters from one of Wales's all-time great players. And his prediction wasn't far off the mark, either.

As I have said, Gareth and I were in harness again quite soon, against New Zealand at Cardiff on 11 November. Another defeat. Oh dear, life at the top didn't seem that wonderful to either of us at the time. But around the corner, a few months later, we were to be part of one of the great thrills in rugby – a Triple Crown winning side, in 1979. Only one point was to separate us from an even bigger thrill, a Grand Slam.

Our first match was against Scotland, at Murrayfield, a graveyard of many Welsh hopes. By half-time we were adrift, 6–13, and then had to play into a stiff breeze. The prospects looked less than rosy. I was soon to discover how good the Welsh forwards of that era were, and we had Scotland back-pedalling for most of the second half. Score by score, point by point, we pulled back the deficit. Suddenly, from being behind, we were level. When you are involved in a hectic match like this, you lose track of time, but I knew that the next score would win the match. It did. The Scottish pack was under a lot of pressure, and were tiring when our forwards put in one more great effort at a five-yard scrummage. We won the ball against the head, wheeled the scrum and with bodies, arms and legs thrashing about over the try-line, I pounced on the loose ball. Steve Fenwick kicked the conversion and we were home.

A month later we beat Ireland 24–21 at the Arms Park, and what a battle the Paddies gave us. The Press, however, were not amused, nor were they impressed. The hero of Murrayfield was panned by all and sundry. They criticised everything I did, except the way I ran on the field. A fortnight later we were off to Paris, the Moulin Rouge, the Eiffel Tower, frog's legs and wine – yes, my first visit. I'd have loved every moment of it, but for one thing. The day before the match the *Western Mail* ran a series of letters from readers which, without exception, were scathing attacks on myself and Gareth. I have never objected to criticism – in fact it is a very good thing, if it is constructive and well intentioned – but I was bitterly upset that at a time when the Welsh team were looking for encouragement before what was obviously going to be their hardest match, our local paper, which always claimed to be an ardent supporter of Welsh rugby, should become the vehicle of morale-sapping attacks. I was only twenty-one, too young, naive maybe, to take the episode in my stride, but even now I have to say I suspect the motives of the person responsible for the untimely publication of those letters.

The match itself was all France. Oddly, we almost won, and could have, but the truth was that we wouldn't have deserved to. I felt I played quite well, scored a try, and was genuinely surprised to win the man-of-the-match award. But if Edinburgh was to be one of my favourite and lucky grounds, Parc de Princes most certainly was not. I was to play there three times. Three defeats. Not that I didn't enjoy playing in that human cauldron.

It was magnificent, frightening in a way, with the noise, the bands, trumpets and horns, the passion and the baying for blood – and that was just the spectators. The French came at us with a fury of starved lions turned loose on the Christians. I'd never experienced anything quite like it on a rugby field, and I was in such a state of shock in that supercharged atmosphere that there were moments I didn't know where I was. After about twenty minutes, I shouted across to Gareth: 'What the bloody hell's the score?' He was convinced I'd had a bump. The match was also my first opportunity to assess Jérome Gallion, the highly rated French scrum-half. I gave him my best attention, and I needed to because he was highly volatile and nippy and possessed a good quick pass. I reckon I must have done well against him because at the end he came up and said: 'Thank you, Terry.'

A week after I'd celebrated my twenty-second birthday we were toasting a Triple Crown and the winning of the Championship. This time the party went on until the early hours. The players weren't the only ones out on the town. We had out-played England in every department and the Arms Park crowd loved it. It was Wales's biggest victory over their oldest enemy since 1905, a 27–3 total boosted by Stevie Fenwick who brought his Championship total to 38 points, equalling Phil Bennett's record. T.H. and W.G.D. had arrived – the papers said so. I'll never understand them.

When I first arrived at Bradford, I renewed contact with an old Cardiff buddy and distant relative, Phil Ford, who was scoring a lot of tries from the wing for Northern. Phil remembers our Triple Crown win very well – he reckons he helped us. I suppose he did. He was one of the ball-boys at Cardiff that afternoon.

England v. Wales matches always held a special appeal for me: something unusual always seemed to occur in them – the Ringer match in 1980; popping out my shoulder in 1982; making my comeback from Lions injury and playing with my old pal, Spikey Watkins, in 1984; and my last Championship appearance in 1985 when I was captain and we won. The rugby and the intense rivalry apart, England was always great off the field. I used to think they picked their players not for their rugby ability but for their social qualities. I don't think you'll find better company anywhere. They pretend they don't take the game seriously, but deep down they love it passionately and want to win just as desperately as any Welshman.

From the viewpoint of satisfaction, however, my favourite opponents were Scotland. I played four matches against them, three of them at Murrayfield, and Wales won each time. I don't want to give the impression that we were always beating the Scots. Not true. Wales lost to them in 1981 (15–6), 1982 (34–18) and 1984 (15–9). Foxy old Holmes; he missed all those matches, because of injury. Generally speaking, it was good to play against Scotland because they concentrated on their own game, and allowed you to play yours. In my time, they were the least defence-minded in the Championship and possessed some fine counter-attacking players like John Rutherford and Jim Renwick. Roy Laidlaw, at scrum-half, was always a handful, too, and I never felt that I completely mastered him in any match. The Scots also turned out a clutch of lean, fast grey-hounds going under the name of loose-forwards, and sometimes I was dumbstruck as one of them loped past me as if I were standing still. The story used to go the rounds that Jim Renwick hated training and was never 100 per cent fit. If that's true, thank goodness for it, because he gave Wales more than enough to think about: he was a footballer in every sense, and in my experience one of the best opportunists. I would like to have got to know Jim well. Trouble was, I had a bit of a difficulty coping with Jim's Border brogue; he sounded to me as if he was chewing razor blades.

In a sense, the final whistle signalled a new beginning. You have to hand it to the Scottish Rugby Union. They know how to lay on a really good after-match banquet. Theirs is easily the most sociable, not merely because of its informality, but because it is organised with the players in mind. A lot of countries seem to regard an international match dinner as an occasion to overload it with alickadoos, committeemen and friends. The function goes on interminably, and many's the time I've nearly fallen asleep as speaker after speaker drones on. The Scots reckon it's the players' night, and of course it is. You tuck in to the haggis and then you're straight on to the Highland wine.

I would love to have won in Paris with Wales, and the same goes for Lansdowne Road. I played in Dublin twice, in 1980 and 1982, and the Irish gave us a right seeing-to. Ollie Campbell was the architect of our downfall each time, garnering 19 points in the two matches, and, if I remember rightly, playing a big part in setting up several of their tries. The 1982 match was sad for other reasons: David Irwin broke his leg and my old pal Geoff Wheel played his last match for Wales.

Apart from the Triple Crown of 1979, easily the best period I had in a Welsh jersey was between February 1983 and March 1985. In that time we lost only once, to France in Paris, and managed to win four times and draw once. The victories

Career Record With Wales

17 June 1978	Australia	Sydney	L 17–19
11 November 1978	New Zealand	Cardiff	L 12–13
1 January 1979	Scotland	Edinburgh	W 19–13
3 February 1979	Ireland	Cardiff	W 24–21
17 February 1979	France	Paris	L 13–14
17 March 1979	England	Cardiff	W 27–3
19 January 1980	France	Cardiff	W 18–9
16 February 1980	England	Twickenham	L 8–9
1 March 1980	Scotland	Cardiff	W 17–6
15 March 1980	Ireland	Dublin	L 7–21
1 November 1980	New Zealand	Cardiff	L 3–23
5 December 1981	Australia	Cardiff	W 18–13
23 January 1982	Ireland	Dublin	L 12–20
6 February 1982	France	Cardiff	W 22–12
6 March 1982	England	Twickenham	L 7–17
5 February 1983	England	Cardiff	D 13–13
19 February 1983	Scotland	Edinburgh	W 19–15
5 March 1983	Ireland	Cardiff	W 23–9
19 March 1983	France	Paris	L 9–16
17 March 1984	England	Twickenham	W 24–15
2 March 1985	Scotland	Edinburgh	W 25–21
16 March 1985	Ireland	Cardiff	L 9–21
30 March 1985	France	Paris	L 3–14
20 April 1985	England	Cardiff	W 24–15
9 November 1985	Fiji	Cardiff	W 40–3

Played 25, Won 13, Drawn 1, Lost 11

included a 24–15 result at Twickenham in 1984, my first win on the ground.

I started my international career with a try and a defeat against Australia in 1978 and I'm very glad to say that I ended it with a try and a huge victory, against Fiji in 1985. The Fiji game was highly satisfactory from a personal viewpoint because I captained a side which played very well, and scored some excellent tries. Remember, the Fijians had just played at Lansdowne Road and all but beat Ireland. A knock on the knee forced me to leave the field, but because Wales had played well the crowd gave me a fantastic reception. Little did they know I would never appear in a Wales jersey again.

15
Touring

If I were blindfolded and stuck a pin into a map of the world, the chances are that it would land somewhere I have been or have flown over *en route* to somewhere else. That is the lot, the fate, of the modern rugby player. He is Columbus, Captain Cook and Sir Francis Chichester – adventurer and traveller. The world is the rugbyman's oyster, and only those, say, with a fear of flying fail to grasp the opportunity. My own travelogue sounds like a Thomas Cook brochure – New Zealand, South Africa, Ireland, Italy, France, Zimbabwe, Thailand, Pakistan, Hong Kong, Japan and Australia, and others. What an experience. What an adventure it has all been.

I've never been envious of anybody's lifestyle, and deep down I can't think of a better place to live than Cardiff. That's home. That's where I want to be, and probably that's where I'll die. But if I had a choice, or some extraordinary circumstances forced me to believe I had to live somewhere else in this big, wonderful world, it'd be Australia. Without a doubt. I'm like Ian Botham. I love it there – particularly Perth and Western Australia. Perth is a really beautiful city with lovely people. And whether you're a Pom or not, when a Western Australian says 'G'day, mate' to a stranger, he does it with a smile, and he means it.

Apart from my wife, Susan, rugby has been the most important thing in my life. It's not just the playing of the game either, but what playing leads to, what it does for you, widening your experience and knowledge. You meet people you'd not normally meet, you go to places that previously were just names in an atlas. A tour is an adventure, a journey on which you can fulfil all your ambitions – the ultimate in self-indulgence. For me, all this was encapsulated in Western Australia, with its sun and sea and the good life. Perth has been described as the Dallas of the southern hemisphere. I think that's to underestimate Perth, although consumerism and hard-nose business obviously played a big part in creating what they have today. After all, there are more millionaires in Perth than in any other Australian city.

On a rugby tour, a lot of places are much of a muchness, hotels and food stodgily similar, so that you don't mind rushing through. When you leave you don't feel you've missed anything. In Perth it's different. I wasn't surprised to learn that the city has more sunshine and a greater number of clear days than any other State capital. It also has the wettest winter, the driest summer, and is the windiest of Australia's cities. They've even got a name for their wind – the 'Fremantle Doctor'. Everything is so clean and tidy, and the air, so sharp and clear, is like breathing champagne.

As Perth was largely rebuilt in the twentieth century, there are many ultra-modern buildings, but they don't seem to dominate the older areas of the city, where the neo-colonial houses look as if they might have been built yesterday. I was told that the old architectural heritage has suffered, which is a pity, for it's these older buildings which help give you a sense of identity, and, strangely, of belonging: no foreign outpost this, for Britons. Cardiff has some impressive public buildings, and a castle, but Perth outranks the Welsh capital with Government House, Parliament House, the Anglican and Roman Catholic cathedrals, the Observatory, which is nearly 100 years old, and the University of Western Australia. Incredibly, there are 6,000 acres of parks and gardens, including King's Park, which has been set aside as a nature reserve, Belmont Park (the horse-racing centre) and the Zoological Gardens. It's a city of character and style, somewhere to stop and contemplate, to relax and enjoy yourself, and wish you could stay longer.

Just down the road from Perth is Fremantle, which before America's Cup fever transformed it, was a sleepy, delightful seaside resort and port doffing its hat to the Indian Ocean and the world. Some rugby visitors even go as far as to contemplate returning – and staying for good. This is an understandable reaction for players conditioned to a winter game; and that applies to most of us. In the northern hemisphere we accept unquestioningly that playing is often an unending battle against elements that are unknown in sunny paradises down under. We know no other rugby life, no other way of getting fit – until we travel somewhere different, like Australia – and then we marvel at what we see. The ice and snow, the rain and cold and biting wind, all seem very, very far away when you stroll along Perth's sun-drenched boulevards, parks and beaches. The sports facilities are superb, as good as I've seen anywhere. Above everything, it's a breeding place for the athlete, the perfect environment in which to train and to play, which helps to explain why today's Wallabies are walloping everyone. The Australian production line turns out athletes who just happen to be rugby players.

Nor is it easy for a player from the Old World, where the game of rugby began, to reconcile himself to the fact that when he tours in Australia he is visiting a country which, apart from Britain, has the longest tradition of playing the game.

When I went there with Wales in 1978, we were touring a country in which rugby was already 150 years old, having been first played on an organised basis by garrison soldiers in 1829. That's only six years after William Webb Ellis took up the ball and ran with it at Rugby School, the alleged starting point of the world's greatest game. By gum, they weren't even playing the game in Wales then.

To put the chronology into even sharper perspective, Australian rugby started fifty years before the foundation of the Welsh Rugby Union. Furthermore, the first two Australian clubs, Sydney University (1864) and Wallaroo (1869), were flourishing before the formation of Wales's oldest club, Neath, which came into being in 1871. My old club, Cardiff (1876), is a mere fledgling on the scroll of club histories.

Australia has developed most remarkably from the humblest and most unpromising of beginnings into a dynamic, confident country of wealth and influence. The modern Australian stands tall and proud because he's entitled to, and we would do well to acknowledge that, not only in rugby terms.

Take, for instance, my favourite part of that vast continent, Western Australia. It is mind-boggling to think that less than 150 years ago this was a beautiful wilderness, teeming with wildlife and untouched by man's civilising influence.

In May 1829 the frigate *Challenger* sailed into the Swan River estuary, and the master, Captain Charles Fremantle, took formal possession of one million square miles of the surrounding territory. He named it Western Australia, the first time the word 'Australia' had been formally used. A garrison was established, and presumably those that manned it were the new country's first rugby players. Colonisation then started in earnest, and about the time that the transportation of convicts to eastern Australia ended, Britain's discards began to be shipped to Western Australia. The first convict ship to appear off the newly established town of Fremantle was the *Scindian*, in June 1850. On board were seventy-five felons and fifty-four guards. In January 1868, the thirty-seventh and last convict ship, the *Hougoumont*, put ashore 279 prisoners. In those nineteen years, a total of 9,668 convicts, all men, were sent to Western Australia. From that breeding stock are today's Australians, who have achieved in a short span of time probably more than any other nation in the world. There are more than a million Western Australians now, including, incidentally, over 7,000 Aborigines. They have turned their climatic advantages to the good in many ways, not the least in rugby – of either code.

I point to these facts merely because there is a widespread view in Britain (which I admit I used to share) that whenever a side from Britain visited Australia we were travelling there not only as missionaries but also because our folks back home expected us to give our country cousins a lesson in the arts and crafts of the game.

This was not true in 1978, nor is it true today. In fact, the reverse is pertinent. In many aspects of rugby, we, the 'older' countries, are the pupils, and the Australians, among others, are the masters. Once in a while – as with the 1971 British Lions in New Zealand and South Africa in 1974 – we prove we are the best in the world. It doesn't happen very often.

By the time this book is published, the World Cup will be

over. I'm normally too cautious a bloke to make predictions, but I wouldn't mind betting that they'll have toasted their heroes and might have had cause to celebrate down in Perth, in Fremantle, Brisbane, Sydney and Wallaroo.

Even if the Aussies didn't get their hands on the William Webb Ellis trophy, they'll have gone very close, that's for sure. Gdonyer, lads.

I'm not sure my love affair with Australia was shared by the other Welsh players on that 1978 tour. Geoff Wheel, for instance, had some reservations. Geoff has a phobia about creepy-crawlies, and once the boys discovered that, they made it their business to remind Geoff that Australia abounded with them. 'Do you know, even their spiders are poisonous – one bite and you're dead!' It's hard to imagine a macho man like Geoff being afraid of anything, but he would have rather faced four Irish forwards than something equally hairy and eight-legged, like *Idiommata blackwalli*, a deadly venomous trapdoor spider which, according to the naturalists among the team, was common in the Perth suburbs. The more the boys warned poor Geoff, the worse he got. By the end of the first couple of weeks in Australia he was positively paranoiac. He'd lock himself into his hotel room and jam up every gap he could find, beneath the door and the windows. Some of the lads considered taking the joke even further, by planting a live specimen in Geoff's bed or bath. The idea was dismissed when they reflected upon the outcome if ever he discovered he'd been the victim of a prank. Murder might have been committed.

Geoff's discomfort naturally proved a source of great amusement for the team, the wicked lot – although many of them felt they needed light relief. The rugby side of the tour was less than satisfactory, for Wales lost four matches, including both Tests.

I'm not one to carp about the opposition and rarely do I knock referees. It seems a futile exercise and never changes the results. However, the WRU management had a point when they protested about the standard of refereeing on that tour. I'd go so far as to say that most of the referees we had were 'homers'. A lot of problems stemmed from different interpretations of the laws. Then there was the callous, brutal assault on Graham Price in the Second Test in Sydney, which ended in his going off with multiple facial fractures. But, ultimately, the biggest handicap Wales had to endure was on the injury front. As the tour progressed players went down like ninepins and we had to cobble a team together for the Second Test. Looking back at that side, I can only wonder at the compromise. J. P. R. Williams played flanker, Alun Donovan was at full-back, and Clive Davis was at No. 8. Oh, yes, Wales had a new scrum-half: yours truly. My first cap: 17 June 1978, a date to remember for many reasons. Gerald Davies, too, will remember that day. It was his forty-sixth and final appearance for Wales, his first as captain. We both scored tries. Mine was very important, because it was the icing on the cake of my Wales début. But for Gerald it was the near-perfect finale – his try was his twentieth for Wales, thus equalling Gareth Edwards's record.

Those few incidents, regrettably, were about the only cause for celebration. Wales were beaten 19–17, the difference made up by a dropped goal by Paul McLean, which even to many local supporters seemed to have passed outside the post. That was the last of many pieces of ill-luck that dogged this my first, and still most memorable, tour.

I have been told that someone not interested in politics is apolitical. I can't think of a better word to describe myself, for politics holds as much appeal for me as diving into a shark-infested pool. I would happily go through the rest of my life maintaining this discreet indifference, but unfortunately, as a sportsman, I cannot avoid becoming embroiled. I'm referring, of course, to my links with South Africa, a country I've toured with both Cardiff and the British Lions.

Let me say at once, I found South Africa a fascinating, lovely country and many South Africans whom I met there were pleasant, affable and fair-minded. The common denominator was rugby, and I suppose if we had been left to our own devices, and ignored by the politicians, the South African trip would be one for pleasant and happy recall. Sadly it was not so. Cardiff long ago stopped filling up the club's archives with letters from outraged anti-Apartheid supporters. You're on the 'black list', I was told, along with other miscreants like Gareth Davies and Alan Phillips. I used to think that in the circumstances this was an oddly inapt phrase.

While I was in South Africa, I did witness events which caused me embarrassment, particularly as I grew up in a multicultural environment. The treatment of black waiters was awful at times, a form of class division I thought had disappeared in the last days of Empire. When I enquired about such attitudes, I realised immediately that not only could I not understand the local viewpoint, but they didn't understand mine either. South Africa has a lot of problems, but they have to sort them out themselves. It is not for sportsmen to be involved, to be exploited in a debate not of their making. I have a few close friends who happen to be black, like Carl Smith and Gerald Cordle, who played with me at Cardiff. They are fiercely against the South African regime and would never play there. That is understandable because black people are black whether they come from Tiger Bay, Brixton, Barbados or the townships in South Africa. But the interesting thing is that neither Gerald nor Carl would ever seek to impose their beliefs upon me, nor would they dream of trying to persuade me not to tour there. They respected my decision to tour and that I went to play rugby.

From a purely rugby standpoint, it is a tragedy that sportsmen in South Africa are prevented from participating in so many sports because of their country's politics. We'll never be able to prove it now, but from my experience of playing out there, I think the South Africans would beat any side in the world. In that respect, rugby is the loser, for we are denied seeing the best.

I enjoyed touring New Zealand, although as with my Lions tour of South Africa, the trip was all too brief. My observations of the game in New Zealand are obviously restricted to my own experience. I admire their will to win, and without the Spring-boks to challenge them, probably they are the best side in the world. They are well coached and extremely well organised at all levels of the game. They train very hard, and their fitness and commitment are admirable. Yet while I found much to admire, I felt that their game generally lacked flair and imagination. Their centres and wings were fast, aggressively so, but it was disappointing not to see a side-step or a body-swerve. As they win a lot – and beat sides in which people like myself played – who's to say their attitude is wrong?

16
Criticism

The general public – and the media, to a certain extent – find it hard to understand that the so-called sports superstar, whatever his image, is nothing more than an ordinary person. He is depicted as leading a life completely different from that of others, never doing anything that *normal* people do. It is absurd, of course, a myth: outside the playing field, which in a sense is his theatre, the playing and the performing stops, and he reverts to a life no different from anyone else's. At least he tries. If he is lucky he succeeds. The superstar still has to work, eat and sleep; he cleans the loo, trims the garden hedge, mends the roof, dries the dishes, worries about the bills and the overdraft. Like everyone else, he falls in love, marries and has rows with his wife, just like the miner, the shepherd, the office-worker, the politician or the high-court judge. He may also be a drinker or a drunkard, honest and kindly, or a cheat, a scrooge or a gambler.

Some sportsmen have a dreadful time living up to – or living down – a reputation away from the activity which has brought them fame. Ian Botham is a good example. It's curious, but those who cheer him hoarse and praise his cricketing brilliance one moment, are tut-tutting with moral indignation the next when some doubtful aspect of his private life emerges or, rather, is dug out by the mud-slingers of Fleet Street. I've met Ian a couple of times, and he is very good company. I like people who call a spade a spade. Ian's certainly one of those. He's a big fan of rugby, and knowledgeable, too; if he'd not been side-tracked into playing football, I have a feeling he might have made an interesting addition to some club's front row. I remember once after a charity do in which we were all involved, Gareth Davies and I took Botham on, as it were, glass for glass. I quit early.

159

Now Gareth can hold his own with most in this respect, but after that session Ian was still going strong, while Gareth, on the way home in the back of the car, wound down the window to count the cat's-eyes. Ian Botham 2, Holmes and Davies 0.

I'm no great tennis fan, but I'm an avid TV viewer when John McEnroe plays, more as one sportsman applauding the skills of another than as an expert on the game. It seems to me that John's lack of self-control on court is a serious defect as a player, but that's all. He may not be as victimised as he sometimes claims, but victim he is in that everyone has placed far too much emphasis on the fiery side of his character, so that almost anything he does, on and off the court, is subject to unfair and unwarranted inspection. I'm told that off-court, in private, he is a smashing guy, courteous and polite and tremendous company. He doesn't bonk the milkman on the head with his racket or even kick the cat. If he did, though, you can bet the cat would be on the phone to the Press straight away!

When I compare my sporting life with sportsmen like Botham and McEnroe, I thank my lucky stars that, with a couple of exceptions, I've escaped the nasties. I've been allowed to lead a relatively normal life outside the game, with few intrusions, no poison-pen letters or threats. Or a bad press. For a lot of sportsmen the outside pressure is difficult to cope with. Some have even quit the game because of it. For me, fortunately, it was never a problem. I accepted and coped with the pressure in my own quiet and restrained way. I would go so far as to say I don't really care what anybody says, or writes about me. I take the pats on the back, and I take the knocks, simple as that. It isn't indifference – probably deference to the inevitable.

I came to terms with being in the public eye, under scrutiny, rather early in my career, which made things a lot easier when, for instance, I found myself much more in the limelight on being made captain of Wales. It is an honour that has in-built responsibilities and obligations, among them direct dealing with the media. I was always very aware that every word I uttered, every comment I made, would be noted and analysed. Caution was a natural by-product of that awareness. The result, of course, is that a captain of Wales often comes over as a bland, noncontroversial character, which isn't bad in itself but can lead to misrepresentation. I'd also like to underline that the WRU policy of allowing the Welsh captain to be the team's spokesman doesn't imply that he is gagged in any way. He is not instructed what to say or what not to say. I point this out because I know a lot of people believe the reverse, and that a lot of unfair criticism of the WRU generally and the coaching-selection set-up stems from this misconception.

Although I sometimes disagreed with their opinions, I found, on the whole, that the representatives of the media were fair and balanced. I got on socially with quite a few of them, but it is hard for a sportsman to become really friendly with a journalist because you can never absolutely trust him. After all, it's his job to find and write stories, and a casual remark in a social atmosphere could land a lot of people in hot water. I'm a bit old-fashioned, I suppose, but I rate loyalty and trust very high in a game which has obvious growing pains in coping with the accompanying pressures of its increased popularity.

If I'm circumspect with the Press, there are others who have to be dealt with quite differently. I suppose every sport has them, but apparently rugby has a peculiar attraction for people the players describe as 'Heavies', an apt coinage if ever there was one. Heavies are a real pain in the bum, who wangle themselves into all sorts of places where you'd never expect them. Over the years, you become quite expert in dealing with them: a smile, or an adroit side-step accompanied by a polite 'excuse me' are the answers to the boor and the loudmouth who insist on your listening to their comments on the game, chapter and verse. Which proves, probably, that I'm pretty laconic and at worst thick-skinned.

During the 1970s, when Welsh and British rugby was at a peak of popularity, the Heavies were out in force. I like the way the players of those days handled them. When confronted, or cornered, the victim would try surreptitiously to attract the attention of another player. 'Rescue me now!' was the insistent message, and he indicated his plight by fingering an ear-lobe – a signal for a nearby player to come rushing up and, on some pretext or another, to drag the poor ear-bashed player away.

Many of these Heavies are true fans of the game, and mostly well-meaning, but, with respect, the last thing any player wants to do after a game is to enter into a long repetitive and boring discussion on the whys and wherefores of the game, whether somebody played well or badly, or whether the referee was right or wrong to award a try.

There is a third category in the list of rugby players' pet hates. He is the foul-mouthed lout, whose courage or audacity is usually in direct proportion to the amount of alcohol consumed. Thankfully I haven't met many of this type, but on a couple of occasions the old hackles have risen. One incident has lodged in my memory for no other reason than that it happened in the presence of my wife.

On 16 March 1985 Wales lost to Ireland 9–21 at the Cardiff Arms Park. Without wanting to take anything away from the Irish that day, because they won well, we really did make a present of the match to them. We outplayed them at forward and had enough possession to have won by the proverbial street. At the end the Welsh dressing-room was a sombre place; the players were more angry with themselves than dispirited. We all knew we'd chucked the game away. As captain, I felt for the boys. After losing like that, though, you don't usually say anything very much. It would either sound carping or patronising.

However, the after-match dinner-dance at the Angel Hotel was good, enjoyable with our wives there, and by the end of the night I don't think anybody begrudged the Irish their victory. The Irish are the best in the world in accepting defeat with grace and a laugh, and they never gloat when they win. It's a tremendous and admirable formula for putting zing into the après-match!

Certainly our spirits had risen by the end of that particular evening, and when Gareth and I, with our wives, decided to unwind a bit further at a local night-club we were in a fairly happy frame of mind. In Cardiff no place is very far from anywhere else, so the four of us strolled a couple of hundred yards from the Angel down to Jackson's Club, which backs on to the Arms Park, in Westgate Street. It was late, very late, but there were still people roaming about, mostly celebrating Irish fans or disconsolate Welsh ones. We were recognised and confronted by one of the latter. It was not a happy meeting.

He was evidently drunk, but no victim of alcoholic amnesia. He hadn't forgotten events earlier in the day, and chancing upon two of the agents of his obvious misery, Gareth and myself, he viewed us with a less than charitable eye. The abusive language was torrid. Without our wives, Gareth and I would normally have shrugged off such an encounter. In some circumstances, we might even have faced up to him, square on as it were, and politely asked him to desist. But because Helen and Susan were with us, the insults were even more upsetting. I'm not quick to anger, but I was absolutely fuming this time, and it took a very great personal effort for me not to go up to the lout and give him a good hiding. Instead, I ushered everyone away, into Jackson's, leaving the yobbo to hurl his abuse into the night sky. We had a few drinks. They tasted bitter and the mood was funereal. The girls were still hurt and upset. I must say, the incident made me wonder what on earth I was doing belonging to a sport, and an amateur one at that, that could evoke such ill-will. It didn't make sense.

17

Future

There can be little doubt that Rugby Union today is at the crossroads. The game which not so long ago was a front-line sport in about a dozen countries has now become a significant leisure activity in more than 120 – incredible considering the game has spread without a supervisory legislative or administrative body to run the sport in global terms. There is also the so-called threat of professionalism casting a dark shadow over everything, including rugby's first World Cup.

The International Board, which has managed rugby's affairs up till now, is effectively a toothless tiger. It may seem hard to believe, but the IB influence has always been very limited, restricted to making changes to the laws of the game. The Board met only occasionally and did little more than tinker inconsequentially with laws that have been part of the game since the 1800s. The IB was neither designed for, nor capable of, administering a world game. A fundamental change of thinking is needed if the IB influence is to be wielded world-wide, if its grasp and control are to be exerted. To cope with the new problems a World Rugby Authority, an administrative body, a secretariat, whatever you like to call it, is indispensable.

I think much of this will have become obvious after the World Cup in 1987, a competition which I imagine most people believe was staged for a twofold purpose: to prove which country is the best in the world and to provide the means for increasing the revenues of the competing nations. I think the World Cup will prove to do more than that. It is likely to be a springboard, a platform for the formation of the WRA, out of which will grow a resolve and strength to resist all threats of professionalism. Once that particular bogy is firmly dealt with, it can concentrate its thinking on promoting the game and helping it to prosper world-wide. Provided a fresh and realistic approach is made with regard to players receiving expenses and the like, I feel sure the danger of professionalism (real or perceived), and the rhetoric which promotes it, will recede into insignificance. Rugby Union will remain amateur, if that's what everybody wants and pro-vided the new governing body is businesslike and resolute.

Viewing events, as it were, from the other side of the fence, it seems to me that Rugby Union faces a fantastic, stimulating challenge, full of exciting prospects. The World Cup was the catalyst.

What interests me more, however, is what we do back home, in Wales in particular, and in Britain generally. Without wishing to over-simplify such a wide-ranging subject, I think we in Britain must make our own game the number-one priority. Let us get our own house in order, and allow the WRA to look after the interests of the rest of the world. There are countries which need help. We don't. We can help ourselves.

I don't think there are many players of my vintage not painfully aware that the standard of British rugby has declined. It doesn't help, either, for the critics to point out how superior, for example, are New Zealand and Australia. This only means that they are ahead of us at the moment; our decline has made their rugby appear better than it really is. We must concentrate on improving, on raising our standards, not by imitating or copying the style and approach of other countries, but by giving our players the chance to express themselves fully in the context of a British game. I'm convinced we already have the players to do just that, and will continue to produce them. It is the system which is at fault: we are bogged down by tradition and tradition-alists, and I feel sure that a new broom, a new attitude, would produce changes for the better.

I'd go so far as to suggest that if we could get our act together in Britain, we'd beat the world, including South Africa, who, as I've said, are probably even better than the All Blacks and the Wallabies. Whether they'll get the chance to prove that in the foreseeable future, though, seems increasingly doubtful.

I wouldn't like it thought that I'm criticising the game in

Britain, or those who administer it. I owe the sport far too much ever to run it down piecemeal. For all its faults and problems, Rugby Union is still a marvellous activity, a superb game, and I can't imagine greater fulfilment for a youngster than to play in a team game such as rugby and enjoy it. No game can match Rugby Union in combining vigorous pleasure on the field and fellowship off it. Nor am I claiming that my suggestions for improvement in our game are the only ones, or even original. They are really personal ideas, thoughts that have occurred to me as my Rugby Union career came to a close and my new challenge with Bradford Northern sharpened my perceptions. If these thoughts stimulate some debate among rugby folk, then perhaps I'll have gone a little way to repay my debt to the game. I've always thought that when people stop thinking about how to improve the game, then that game is on the way to its own funeral.

The solution, I believe, rests entirely with the four home unions, who should carefully scrutinise the game in Britain and come up with an alternative to a system which is both archaic and divisive. British rugby is based on a traditional formula, with many various factions, self-interest and self-indulgence, which in real terms leaves us tottering along like an old donkey in a race for thoroughbreds. The British system simply isn't good enough for us to compete at the highest level. With a few exceptions, we've been going downhill since 1971, and although the warning signs have blared out periodically, people seem disinclined, or too apathetic, to heed them.

It seems to me that we have now reached the point at which the choice is straightforward: either we in Britain accept that we could be condemned forever as second-rate, or we try to do something about it.

I'm not suggesting change for change's sake, and I cannot visualise a substantial improvement if only one or two countries grasp the nettle. All four home unions should be involved and must co-operate. England, Ireland, Scotland and Wales have got to work at the problem together, to combine their talents in both a playing and an administrative sense to provide the solution. We're trailing Australia, France, New Zealand and

South Africa at the moment, and if we're not careful we'll also be left behind by some of the emergent rugby countries. Finishing last is bad enough. What happens if we're nudged aside and find ourselves not in the race at all, which is a possibility that might not be as absurd as some might think? I know Romania took a bit of a pasting when they played Ireland in the autumn of 1986, but their progress, like that of Argentina, Canada and the USA, is impressive. If you add other countries, such as Italy and the Soviet Union, and their game continues to improve at the same rate that ours declines, the consequences are ominous.

It's pretty obvious that what I'm advocating is that the four home unions join together to produce a British Isles side. I know we already have the Lions, who are brought together every now and then to tour abroad. But I am suggesting that the Lions play at *home* as well, and regularly stage Test matches against incoming major touring sides at the Arms Park, Lansdowne Road, Murrayfield and Twickenham. If you think a ticket for Wales v. England at Cardiff is difficult to obtain, imagine what it would be like to get one for the Lions v. the All Blacks at Twickenham!

The Lions playing at home, of course, is only part of this Terry Holmes fairy-story, the top of the pyramid in every sense. Because, for that to happen, almost the whole superstructure of British rugby would have to be modified. This is where the Grand Plan might find its most vehement opposition, for such a change would threaten to undermine the most jealously defended element in the game in the British Isles – the club tradition.

In Wales, particularly when the national XV isn't doing very well, we often seek explanations in a most curious way, using the players like ping-pong balls, bouncing them between the twin evils of self-denigration and outrageous criticism. After that comes the solace: 'Ah, well, we still have the best club system in the world.' As one who used to be very much part of that club system (and agreed with the 'we're best' view), it might seem faintly absurd to argue against something which probably couldn't be proved anyway. But, best or not, what, in effect, are the clubs and their traditions currently *achieving* for Wales? I'm

167

sorry to say it, but I suggest very little. In fact, the system as it stands is possibly one of the causes of the decline in Welsh international standards, and because traditionally Wales has played such an important part in British rugby, it may be the indirect reason for lower standards throughout the rest of the British Isles.

This is not the fault of the clubs themselves, except perhaps in the hotly debated area of the overplaying of individuals and the arbitrary increase in fixtures.

What is required, in my view, is a radical and highly important change in the way we run the game in the British Isles. In the first place, the clubs should have less influence and play a smaller role in relation to producing international players. Although there are exceptions, in most cases the gap between club rugby and international rugby is far too wide, and it is that gap which leaves the British game floundering. If we have any chance of matching the superior rugby nations, we need somehow to bridge that gap, to build stepping-stones between club and cap. As in New Zealand and South Africa, and to a lesser extent Australia, we need to infuse quality and competition so that players are better prepared for the international arena. The only way I can visualise this happening is by introducing a kind of provincial structure throughout Britain. This might not be all that of a quantum leap, because in parts of the British Isles, such as Ireland, a provincial competition already exists. There is also the county and divisional championship in England and Wales.

As these competitions stand at the moment, however, and without wishing to detract from the good intentions of their proponents, it has to be said that they are not, over all, of high enough quality. As far as most players are concerned, the best rugby they can play is at club level – although many will acknowledge that this still leaves them tellingly ill-equipped for international rugby. At the moment, the incentive is simply not there for the best players in each country to want to play for provincial sides. Clubs have always exercised priority. But if these provincial sides were reconstructed and regarded as the only yardstick by which play standards were measured, they would provide the basis for selecting British Isles teams. The effect would be quite dramatic, not only in the attitude of the players, but in raising playing standards throughout the British Isles. This is very much the situation in New Zealand and South Africa, and I'm sure is the chief reason that they have dominated the game for so long. Players in those countries are involved with clubs, but at a very limited level. If he is good enough, the overseas player's aspirations are geared towards gaining selection for his province and thereafter for his country. He also participates in far fewer matches than his British counterpart, who is often overplayed and jaded before the international season starts. Injuries are a by-product of overplaying, and there is much to be said for creating a situation whereby players concentrate on their physical and mental fitness rather than run risks playing twice a week, week in and week out.

If the British game were to be organised on a provincial basis, it would not be of much use unless it were strictly competitive. By this I mean a provincial championship, with the top sides from the four home unions competing against one another. They would also be required to play against the incoming touring sides, which is what happens when the Lions tour New Zealand and South Africa and meet the best provincial teams. A provincial championship would assume enormous importance, for it would provide high-class, quality competition for the best players in Britain and would enable the Lions selectors to run the rule over them, the end object of the exercise being Test matches against incoming touring sides. As touring sides traditionally play in the British Isles in the early part of the season, there would be no interference with the domestic international scene. In fact, I'm convinced that a provincial championship and Lions Test matches would tune up players far better for the Five Nations. The improvement in playing and fitness standards would be across the board, and then, only then, would British rugby be able to face and match the best that the rest of the world has to offer.

I do not, by the way, visualise a British provincial championship totally dominating the domestic scene, nor need it adversely affect the role of the clubs. As I see it, the clubs would benefit directly from the increased income that a provincial championship would generate, so enabling them to curtail their already overlong fixture lists without loss of revenue. Most senior clubs insist that they cannot cut their fixture lists because of the need to raise money for running costs; others are reluctant to drop fixtures, some of which have been played since the last century. All these clubs admit to the overplaying problem, yet few make any real effort to tackle it. The clubs have to be persuaded that they would get more out of their players if they were not so overburdened. The clubs should aim for quality rather than quantity, and would have an important role as 'feeders' to provincial sides. Furthermore, they would, of course, benefit in the sense that when a player's provincial duties are over he would rejoin his club, presumably as a better-equipped player, eager to contribute to his club's fortunes.

This brings me to another problem which Rugby Union has to face – the threat of professionalism. For the life of me, I don't know why the game's administrators have got themselves into such a twist over this. The plain truth is that *Rugby Union players do not want to be paid for playing*. They don't want the game to become professional. I've spoken to hundreds of players on this subject during my time with Cardiff and Wales. Not one of them has expressed any interest in being paid to play – although I can understand that some of our colonial cousins, frustrated by amateurish attitudes over legitimate expenses and broken-time payments, might easily be tempted by agencies outside the game to accept money. That's human nature. If someone comes up with cash for, say, a pirate tour, there are not many players who would say 'no'. Now, if things were different – and I hope they change in this respect – and the top players were treated rather better than they have been, then at a stroke you would wipe away all temptations.

I refer to expenses and payments for activities outside playing. I see no reason why the game's guardians should not change their deep-rooted attitudes over such matters. The game is *not* professionalised because players' needs are catered for; nor would there be any damage if certain players, benefiting from their status and popularity, were to accept cash for, say, appearing on TV, opening supermarkets, or even writing books.

170

I'm not suggesting that players who, like me, have turned professional, should be allowed back in the amateur game; but there are other things they can offer, apart from playing, in the autumn of their career. In recent years particularly, dozens of top players have been lost to the game because antiquated laws demanded that they be ostracised.

Let's look at an example. You would have to go a long way to discover somebody more loyal to his club and country than John Perkins, the Pontypool lock. Perky played over 500 matches for his club and eighteen for Wales. But this service to the game entailed sacrifices and cost him money. When Perky trained and squadded he missed work and, as a self-employed man, when he didn't work he wasn't earning. Certainly he had his fun and enjoyment, but at what cost? Has the game the right to ask any player to deprive his family? Expecting a player to lose out financially is wrong. Perky – and players like him – should have been recompensed. He should also have been allowed to cash in on his status with activities outside the game itself; in a way, that would have more than compensated. Perky, one of the great characters in the game, used to grin and bear his financial losses on behalf of his country. Now that his international career is over, he'll have time to reflect whether the sacrifice was really worth it. I maintain that he and players like him should never be treated in that way, particularly as in relative terms the game has more than enough money adequately to cope with genuine cases of hardship or loss of income. Perky isn't alone in that respect, either. Many, many players give more to the game than they can legitimately afford, and frequently face a dilemma as a consequence. A lot of them give up playing. Others turn to Rugby League. Whilst complaining about the player drain, the people running the game never seem to consider the players themselves who, let's be frank, give more of their time and put in more relative effort than anyone did in the past. If yesterday's players – the administrators of today – start by recognising that one fundamental, I'm sure that changes will be made. They have to be.

It occurs to me that one obvious way of recompensing players who have given a lot to the game is to award them a testimonial match or season, as is done in cricket. Many long-serving players reach the end of their career and the only thing they have to look forward to is perhaps a farewell dinner, at which they will be presented with a modest gift from the club. Such occasions are part of the great tradition of the game, and I'd be the last person to suggest that they cease. However, in this day and age, when very few people can be assured of their job and their future, a testimonial match would in my view represent a more realistic tribute. In my time at Cardiff, for instance, I can think of up to a dozen players who would have merited a testimonial. And what sort of crowd would such a match pull in? I'd wager we'd have a full house at the Arms Park every time – and if all the proceeds from, say, a 10,000 to 16,000 crowd, were to go to the player, it would obviously be well worth staging. The public would certainly support such a gesture, particularly if they knew that the proceeds were destined as a tribute to a long and loyal servant of the club. The fans would want to contribute, I'm sure. Nor would it cost the club a penny, which makes the suggestion that more attractive. Treasurers have an in-built distaste for spending a club's money for anything other than official reasons!

I suppose people will now ask whether, had I been given a testimonial at Cardiff, I would have turned professional. Indeed, would other players have resisted the lure of playing for money if they knew that their club would be staging a testimonial on their behalf? It is a difficult question to answer, certainly in my case, for I had very strong ties with just one club, whereas lots of players have switched clubs often during their careers, and therefore might not 'qualify' because of a relatively short period of service at that particular club.

I put forward the idea of testimonials fully realising that I might be touching off a highly controversial time-bomb, or at least prodding one of the game's tenderest spots. Testimonials, in fact, are not new. There have been several attempts to establish them as a way of rewarding players and, every time, the idea has sparked off bitter and prolonged squabbling within the game. The most notable example of this was way back in 1896 and concerned the man regarded as rugby's first superstar, Arthur Gould. The Newport and Wales centre, an engagingly

172

handsome figure and a fine player, was an attraction wherever he played and his popularity was such that when he announced his retirement at the beginning of the 1896–7 season, after twenty-seven appearances in a Welsh jersey, a testimonial fund was set up on his behalf. It was soon oversubscribed by a grateful Welsh public. The WRU, wishing to recognise Gould's outstanding contribution to their affairs, heartily endorsed the testimonial. Their president, Sir John Llewellyn, formally presented Gould with the deeds of a house in Newport, which was purchased from the proceeds of the fund. But while the whole of Wales was celebrating a hero, on the other side of Offa's Dyke there were dark mutterings and accusations of professionalism. Threats were issued, and they were not empty ones either. Ireland and Scotland flatly refused to play Wales in 1897 and England only fulfilled its fixture after much soul-searching late in the season. Scotland, ardent opponents of anything which smacked of pro-fessionalism – and the Gould testimonial in their eyes was just that – widened the rift even further. They would not play Wales in 1898 either. It was a very serious and damaging dispute, and although it was eventually patched up, the cause thereafter became a taboo subject within the game. Testimonials became a dirty word, unmentionable in the corridors of power of a pristinely amateur game. We are left with the legacy of that dispute today. Only history can judge whether Rugby Union has shot itself in the foot by its implacable opposition to a scheme which may well have enriched the game in every sense. Dare I suggest it, but surely it's about time this particular skeleton was removed from the cupboard and given a good rattling?

I always counted myself lucky that when I was firmly established career-wise, I was comparatively well-off. Rugby was my life but I lost little financially because of my total involvement in the game. I didn't expect anything back from the game; nor, I might add, did I get it. Still, there were moments when I was exasperated at the penny-pinching that prevailed.

I can recall an example of this following the Wales v. Fiji match in 1985, my last appearance for Wales. In the hotel, The Angel, I ordered a cup of tea and a few sandwiches. Perfectly normal request, nothing extravagant, even for someone who's just captained his country. Lo and behold, the next morning the hotel presented me with a bill for my après-match snack. 'I'm not paying his,' I declared. 'It should be down to the WRU.' No, the hotel assured me, there were no extras. The WRU had issued firm instructions on that point. They were paying for bed and breakfast; anything else the players required – even the captain – they had to pay for themselves. Up to that point, I'd always had a fairly high regard for the WRU and generally had got on well with them. In many ways they treated players extremely well. But the incident proved just how much they were lacking in man-management. It was petty and irksome, and I have to admit I felt less than pleased. It underlined the need for the appointment of a middleman, whose job would be to report to the WRU on the players' requirements; someone who could relate to the players and make the powers-that-be aware of the niggling and frustrating little problems that continually crop up. Players realise that today Rugby Union is a big commercial business from which they gain little save their own enjoyment. That's the way it has always been, we are told, and that's the way it must stay. I hope not.

When my Rugby League days are over, I firmly intend to return to Wales and, in some small way perhaps, I hope to put something back into the game of Rugby Union, which has given me so much. As the rules stand at the moment that'll be impossible. I can't teach, coach or help any player or team because I am a professional. In theory I wouldn't even be allowed to coach, say, a lad of my own in the back garden. If he were to join a small local club in Cardiff and I wanted to try to help them, the laws wouldn't allow me. Of all the absurdities in the game, I think this is the most retrogressive. I'm not saying I'd have a great deal to offer, except enthusiasm. But what of other outlaws like David Watkins, Gareth Edwards, Barry John, Gerald Davies, and, in England, Bill Beaumont and Fran Cotton? I ask: can Rugby Union really afford to lose these great players' obvious talents, their experience and influence, simply because of a rule that was drawn up in a different age by people who could have had no conception of how the game would develop and change?

It is really about time that Rugby Union began to examine its self-imposed restrictions. It should recognise that the game needs all the help it can get.

In my heart, although I hope for radical changes, I don't really expect them. When my playing days are over, I reckon I shall knot my blue and black scarf around my neck and satisfy myself with standing on the terraces at the Arms Park, just like I did when I was a schoolboy. That's all I'll be able to do. Still, once a fan, always a fan . . . nothing will change that.

Index

Picture Acknowledgements

Author's Collection: p. 2 top, p. 3 below left, p. 8 top, p. 9 top, p. 10 below, p. 12 below, p. 13 top. *Bradford Telegraph and Argus*: p. 15 top. Mike Brett: p. 14 top, p. 14 below. Colorsport: p. 5, p. 9 below, p. 11 below. George P. Herringshaw/Associated Sports Photography: p. 1, p. 7 below, p. 8 below, p. 16. *Sunday Mirror*: p. 10 top. Bob Thomas: p. 7 top, p. 13 below. *Western Mail and Echo*, Cardiff: p. 2 below right, p. 4 top, p. 6, p. 11 top, p. 12 top. Elwyn White: p. 4 below.